Beyond Shifting Wealth

PERSPECTIVES ON DEVELOPMENT RISKS
AND OPPORTUNITIES FROM THE GLOBAL SOUTH

This work is published under the responsibility of the Secretary-General of the OECD. The opinions expressed and arguments employed herein do not necessarily reflect the official views of the member countries of the OECD or its Development Centre.

This document, as well as any data and map included herein, are without prejudice to the status of or sovereignty over any territory, to the delimitation of international frontiers and boundaries and to the name of any territory, city or area.

Please cite this publication as:
OECD (2017), *Beyond Shifting Wealth: Perspectives on Development Risks and Opportunities from the Global South*, OECD Publishing, Paris.
http://dx.doi.org/10.1787/9789264273153-en

ISBN 978-92-64-27314-6 (print)
ISBN 978-92-64-27315-3 (PDF)

In an integrated global economy, a number of global risks and challenges – from climate change to financial crises to increasing inequality – require coordinated international responses. While risks can be global in that they may affect many countries across multiple continents, the impact in reality may be felt more or less severely in specific places. This has implications on the likelihood, form and effectiveness of international co-operation. For effective international co-operation and action, it is therefore vital to understand the risks and challenges facing us as well as how they are perceived by different countries and actors within the global system.

The OECD Development Centre consistently has sought to scout out emerging trends and issues that require policy responses. Its work on shifting wealth – tracking the growing weight of emerging economies in the global economy – was one such issue that came to define its narrative on development over the last years. The Centre also plays a unique role within the OECD by bridging different policy communities in advanced, emerging and developing economies, thanks to its membership that brings together OECD countries with countries at different stages of development.

This anthology continues in this spirit and contributes to two of the Centre's core objectives: to identify and frame issues that are critical to the development dialogue and to mobilise development knowledge to influence OECD thinking. It is part of the Centre's 2015-16 programme of work to better understand global phenomena and how they impact development to support countries in formulating better development strategies and in enhancing international co-operation to secure global public goods and fight global public "bads".

Specifically, the anthology seeks to anticipate the major global risks and challenges looking forward to the next 15 years. It gathers ideas for solutions and policy responses to mitigate the risks and address the challenges. It brings together contributions from academics, development practitioners and thought leaders from emerging and developing economies to help inform the OECD and the wider development community's thinking. The articles in this anthology represent the authors' views and perspectives. As such, it is the anthology's intention to provide a basis for dialogue and exchange on the national and collective responses that are needed to deal with the global risks and challenges that developing countries and we all face.

Mario Pezzini

Director, OECD Development Centre,
and Special Advisor to the OECD Secretary-General on Development

Acknowledgements

Beyond Shifting Wealth: Perspectives on Development Risks and Opportunities from the Global South was edited by Sam Mealy and Martha Baxter of the OECD Development Centre as part of the Global Risks project supervised by Carl Dahlman, Special Advisor, and under the direction of Mario Pezzini, Director. The editors would like to thank Shane Senecal-Tremblay for his contributions to the writing and help with translation, and Djeneba Doumbia and Melody Chang, Development Centre trainees, who contributed background research and literature reviews in the early stages of the project. The editors would also like to thank Vararat Atisophon for her statistical support. The Development Centre's publications team, led by Delphine Grandrieux, turned the draft into a publication.

The anthology is based on a collection of articles from Hussein Al-Majali, Ahmad Alili, Vugar Bayramov, Debapriya Bhattacharya, Neuma Grobbelaar, Alan Hirsch, Gilbert Houngbo, Tian Huifang, René N'Guettia Kouassi, Donald Mmari, Sarah Sabin Khan, Samir Saran, Vivan Sharan, Karen Van Rompaey, Sanjayan Velautham and Andrea Vignolo.

The editors are grateful to many OECD Development Centre colleagues for their feedback and comments: Federico Bonaglia, Deputy Director (acting), Bathylle Missika, Head of Unit, Partnerships and Networks, Alexandre Kolev, Head of Unit, Social Cohesion, Arthur Minsat, Head of Unit (acting), Europe, Middle East, Africa, Rita Da Costa, Policy Advisor, Director's Office, Linda Smiroldo Herda, Editor and Speechwriter, Director's Office, Juan De Laiglesia, Senior Economist, Multi-Dimensional Country Reviews, Alexander Pick, Economist, Social Protection, Ian Brand-Weiner, Policy Analyst, Youth Inclusion, Rodrigo Deiana, Junior Policy Analyst, Europe, Middle East, Africa, Kate Eklin, Junior Policy Analyst, EMnet, Derek Carnegie, Economist, Asia. The editors are also grateful to Daniel Quadbeck, Project Manager, Eurasia, OECD Global Relations Secretariat, for his useful feedback.

The editors would also like to thank Henri-Bernard Solignac-Lecomte, Head of Division (acting), Senior Communications Manager, OECD Development Cluster, Carlos Conde, Head of Division, OECD Global Relations Secretariat, Marie-Estelle Rey, Senior Policy Analyst, OECD Global Relations Secretariat, Joel Boutroue, Advisor, Regional Co-operation, OECD Development Centre, Thang Nguyen, Junior Policy Analyst, OECD Development Centre, and Florian Kitt, International Energy Association for their suggestions for contributors.

Table of contents

Figures

Tables

Follow OECD Publications on:

http://twitter.com/OECD_Pubs

http://www.facebook.com/OECDPublications

http://www.linkedin.com/groups/OECD-Publications-4645871

http://www.youtube.com/oecdilibrary

http://www.oecd.org/oecddirect/

Acronyms and abbreviations

ACE	ASEAN Centre for Energy
AEC	ASEAN Economic Community
AQAP	Al-Qaeda in the Arabian Peninsula
ASEAN	Association of Southeast Asian Nations
AU	African Union
AUC	African Union Commission
BMZ	Federal Ministry for Economic Co-operation and Development of Germany
BRICS	Brazil, Russian Federation, India, China, South Africa
BRIICS	Brazil, Russian Federation, India, Indonesia, China, South Africa
CABRI	Collaborative Africa Budget Reform Initiative
CAGR	Compound annual growth rate
CEO	Chief Executive Officer
CIS	Commonwealth of Independent States
CPD	Centre for Policy Dialogue
DAC	Development Assistance Committee
DCD	Development Co-operation Directorate
ERIA	Economic Research Institute for ASEAN and East Asia
EU	European Union
FDI	Foreign direct investment
GCC	Gulf Co-operation Council
GDP	Gross Domestic Product
GIZ	Deutsche Gesellschaft für Internationale Zusammenarbeit
GVCs	Global Value Chains
GNI	Gross National Income
HDI	Human Development Index
HIPC	Highly Indebted Poor Countries
ILC	International Labour Conference
ILO	International Labour Organization
IMF	International Monetary Fund
IPoA	Istanbul Programme of Action
IPCC	International Panel on Climate Change
IRENA	International Renewable Energy Agency
ISIC	International Standard Industrial Classification
LAC	Latin America and the Caribbean
LDCs	Least Developed Countries
LED	Light-emitting diode
MDGs	Millennium Development Goals
MENA	Middle East and North Africa
NDB	BRICS New Development Bank
NDCs	Nationally determined contributions

ODA	Official Development Assistance
OECD	Organisation for Economic Co-operation and Development
OPEC	Organization of the Petroleum Exporting Countries
ORF	Observer Research Foundation
PPP	Public Private Partnership
PPP	Purchasing Power Parity
REPOA	Research on Poverty Alleviation, Tanzania
SAIIA	South African Institute of International Affairs
SDGs	Sustainable Development Goals
SEZs	Special Economic Zones
SMEs	Small and medium-sized enterprises
SSCI	Social Sciences Citation Index
STEM	Science, Technology, Engineering and Mathematics
SWTS	School to work transition surveys
TOSSD	Total official support for sustainable development
TPES	Total Primary Energy Supply
UNCTAD	United Nations
UNDP	United Nations Development Programme
UNECA	United Nations Economic Commission for Africa
UNU-Wider	United Nations University World Institute for Development Economics Research
WEF	World Economic Forum
WTO	World Trade Organization

Since the 2000s, economic growth in developing countries generally has been robust, contributing to the phenomenon of *shifting wealth* – the increasing economic weight of developing countries in the world economy – and improved livelihoods. Despite this shift in the global economic centre of gravity, several middle-income countries are not growing fast enough to converge with advanced countries by 2050. Slowing convergence is one factor contributing to a gloomier development prognosis for the next 15 years. Weakening global demand, partly caused by slowing growth in the People's Republic of China (hereafter, China), is hampering the growth prospects of many developing countries. Rising interest rates could fuel volatility in emerging economies' currency, bond and stock markets, and as rates rise, debt-service costs increase. Access to international finance may become increasingly difficult for many developing countries. These challenges will be exacerbated by rapid demographic transitions, urbanisation, premature deindustrialisation, digitalisation and automation, and the rising incidence of climate-related shocks.

Situated within this context, and the ambitious 2030 Sustainable Development Goals (SDGs) agenda, the Development Centre devised this anthology to stimulate discussion on the new global environment. The anthology collects the perspectives of thought leaders from developing and emerging economies, offering their views and solutions on the most pressing global development challenges over the next 15 years.

Perspectives and key findings

Four major global risks emerge as particularly pressing for developing countries: diversifying economies in the context of a more constrained macro environment; the spectre of jobless growth in a period of rapid demographic change and inequality; transitioning to low-carbon economies as energy demands increase and energy security risks intensify; and generating new and improved forms of development co-operation.

Structural transformation in a new macro environment

Diversifying developing economies that are over-reliant on extractives and agriculture will be a major challenge, especially in the context of premature deindustrialisation.

- **Alan Hirsch** contends that growth in sub-Saharan Africa has slowed in recent years because of two main economic policy risks: capital account and fiscal deficits, and high levels of inequality. Several positive signs exist however, including rising agricultural productivity in many sub-Saharan African countries, the growth of small and medium-sized enterprises (SMEs), the recent surge in infrastructure investment, and improvements in health and education.

- Writing about structural transformation in the United Republic of Tanzania (hereafter, Tanzania), **Donald Mmari** calls on policy makers to focus on improving farm-level productivity and strengthening agricultural markets; prioritising budgets and policy incentives to agro-industry and value addition to primary production; and implementing policy measures to raise the productivity of informal enterprises by enhancing their access to resources and markets, and legal identity and rights.

- **Neuma Grobbelaar** outlines five key game changers for Africa that will help accelerate progress toward the SDGs: managing the impact of climate change and moving away from a carbon intensive growth path; addressing the infrastructure gap and the role of domestic resource mobilisation; tackling the digital divide; accelerating land reform; and using migration as a positive driver of development.

- **Vugar Bayramov and Ahmad Alili** note the dependence of Azerbaijan on natural oil and gas reserves over the past 15 years. Falling commodity prices jeopardise its development model. To forge a bright future, they argue Azerbaijan must lessen its dependency on commodities and larger neighbours by increasing its activity within the EU Eastern Partnership and liberalising its economy.

Inclusive societies

Building inclusive societies – in the context of rapid demographic change, jobless growth, rising informality and growing inequality – will be a major challenge facing emerging and developing countries.

- **René N'Guettia Kouassi** contends that growing inequality between countries is the key development challenge over the coming 15 years. Such inequality perpetuates various problems such as conflicts and the migration crisis. Countries should improve social protection programmes to reduce inequality.

- **Gilbert Houngbo** recommends a variety of policy options to encourage the transition of youth from the informal to formal economy, including pro-employment macroeconomic policies; education and training that facilitate the school-to-work transition and correct skills mismatches; and labour market policies that favour employment of disadvantaged youth.

- **Samir Saran** and **Vivan Sharan** stress India's rapidly growing working-age population and encourage policy makers to leverage a "new formality" to absorb these workers into gainful employment. To achieve this, they highlight such factors as the potential of technology to digitally identify each worker, the need to guarantee a reasonable level of income and security, and the importance of the availability of health and life insurance coverage as well as safe working conditions.

- **Hussein Al-Majali** argues that the critical challenge for the Middle East and North Africa (MENA) region is to channel the energy of disaffected Arab youth into "active citizenship". This must be predicated on meaningful employment. Al-Majali recommends that policy makers engage in "prototyping and scaling of solutions customised to local environments" as blanket policies will not work in this increasingly complex policy environment.

Energy and environment

Climate change is the greatest existential threat to humanity in the 21st century, the burden of which falls disproportionately on developing and emerging countries. This topic explores the risks and challenges associated with reconciling growing energy demands, energy security and the transition to low-carbon economies.

- **Sanjayan Velautham** outlines the ASEAN community's challenge of overcoming the "energy trilemma": finding the optimal balance between energy security, environmental sustainability and economic competitiveness. Diversifying energy options will be crucial to achieving this balance.

- **Tian Huifang** argues that the BRICS (Brazil, the Russian Federation, India, China, South Africa) should take policy action in several areas to transition to a low-carbon future, including: following through on the Paris Agreement and regularly renewing nationally determined contributions; promoting strong climate mitigation policies to incentivise the private sector to move to renewables (carbon pricing, targeted investment incentives, etc.); and integrating green finance measures into national development strategies.

New forms of development co-operation

One of the major challenges developing countries face is finding new and improved forms of development co-operation in the context of the SDGs. This topic explores whether Official Development Assistance (ODA), as currently determined, remains fit for purpose, and the risk Least Developed Countries (LDCs) face in being left behind in the SDGs agenda.

- To mitigate the risk of LDCs being left behind, **Debapriya Bhattacharya and Sarah Sabin Khan** propose three key policy areas on which to focus: increased financial resources and access to technology and support for capacity building from the international community; enhanced protection from various systemic risks; and enabling domestic reforms to complement international support measures.
- **Andrea Vignolo and Karen Van Rompaey** argue that ODA will continue to play a role in development co-operation but graduation criteria should be broadened to include other multi-dimensional measures of well-being and sustainability beyond gross national income (GNI) and an alternative timeframe, according to the universality of the 2030 Agenda.

Chapter 1

Overview: development prospects in a new global context

This overview chapter provides a scan of the major risks and challenges that developing and emerging economies may face looking forward. It first gives an overview of the development context over the past 15 years. The chapter then examines major development trends over the coming 15 years, including: the end of the commodity super cycle, access to financial markets, demographic transitions, job creation, urbanisation, climate change and conflict and security. The chapter finishes with a roadmap to the rest of the anthology that summarises the key messages from the anthology's contributors.

The period from 2000-15 was generally a favourable one for developing countries, marked by the phenomenon of shifting wealth: the increasing economic weight of developing countries in the world economy (OECD, 2014). Despite the financial crisis of 2008-09 and resulting economic recession, most developing countries experienced rapid economic growth, convergence between the advanced and emerging economies speeded up, and global livelihoods improved.

The prognosis for the next 15 years is more pessimistic, however. Weakening global demand, partly caused by slowing growth in the People's Republic of China (hereafter, China) will hamper the growth prospects of many developing countries. The prospect of the United States further raising interest rates fuels fears of volatility in emerging economies' currency, bond, and stock markets, and as rates rise, debt-service costs increase. Twenty-eight developing countries with a total population of over 2 billion are projected to exceed the income threshold for Overseas Development Assistance (ODA) eligibility over the period until 2030, and will need to foster new forms of development co-operation and secure other sources of financing (Sedemund, 2014). These challenges will be intensified by rapid demographic transitions, migration, urbanisation, digitalisation and automation, and the rising incidence of climate related shocks, amongst other trends Furthermore, evidence suggests that traditional, development models, typically export-oriented industrialisation, may no longer be appropriate as premature deindustrialisation becomes the norm across developing regions: South Asia is the only region that has experienced an increase in the share of manufacturing in total employment and in GDP since 1990 (Tregenna, 2015).

These challenges will affect developing countries differently. China's slowdown and the end of the commodity super cycle is particularly damaging for commodity exporters. Least developed countries (LDCs) represent a significant portion of these and are least capable of diversifying their economies. Premature deindustrialisation is especially harmful in Latin America and sub-Saharan Africa, where employment in manufacturing as a share of total employment was already low. Job creation could be problematic for sub-Saharan African countries, where the working-age population will approximately double in the next 15-20 years. The negative effects of climate change pose greatest risks for island nations and low-lying countries such as Bangladesh.

This anthology takes an overtly forward-looking perspective in order to anticipate global risks and challenges over the next 15 years and how they might affect countries' development prospects. A burgeoning literature on global risks exists already, perhaps best characterised by the World Economic Forum's annual Global Risks report (WEF, 2016). This anthology aims to complement and expand on this literature by providing an array of forward-looking perspectives from the global South on global risks and challenges. It assembles the contributions of a variety of thought leaders, development practitioners and policy makers from emerging and developing countries to help inform the OECD and broader global community's dialogue on development. It builds on previous and ongoing Development Centre work conducted on global livelihoods and the shifting wealth phenomenon.

The Development Centre conceives of development as a multi-dimensional process with the ultimate measure being people's well-being. Economic growth of course plays a crucial role in driving certain dimensions of development but other outcomes of well-being are loosely or even negatively related to aggregate incomes (OECD, 2013a). Furthermore, people's subjective evaluations of their prospects do not necessarily correspond with their income levels: people in low- and middle-income countries are actually more optimistic about their futures than those in high-income countries (OECD, 2015a). The Development Centre challenges conceptions of development based solely on country-income categories (OECD, 2016a).

Thus, new approaches to development and development co-operation are needed for developing countries to improve their wellbeing, access finance, create employment, and enhance their resilience. In addition, further progress is needed to re-conceptualise development and how it is measured in this changed context: more holistic and multi-dimensional metrics than GDP, such as the OECD Better Life Index, the UNDP Human Development Index (HDI), and the Social Progress Index, should be iterated upon and promoted.

The remainder of this overview provides the Centre's perspective on the new global context and the challenges it poses. It is intended to stimulate questions, discussion on the new global political economy and on the concept of development, while identifying potential policy solutions across a range of thought leaders from emerging and developing economies. It is structured in four sections: first, it briefly reviews the development context over the past 15 years and how development has been framed over this period; second, it argues that the next 15-year period will be significantly more challenging; third, it provides some thoughts on policy proposals and solutions for these challenges; fourth and finally it provides a roadmap to the remainder of the anthology, including its main messages. Beyond this overview chapter, the articles in this anthology neither represent the positions of the Development Centre nor the OECD, but are solely the authors' own views.

2000-2015: A generally favourable development context

Since the 2000s, economic growth in developing countries has been robust, contributing to the phenomenon of shifting wealth and massively improved livelihoods under the framework of the Millennium Development Goals (MDGs). Many developing economies have been growing faster than advanced countries, leading to a shift in the global economic centre of gravity (Figure 1.1). This shift has been driven largely by China. China's strong demand for commodities – including energy, metals and agricultural products – led to a commodity price boom, fuelling growth in many developing countries that produce these commodities. The resultant growth contributed to strong progress in improving global livelihoods and toward achieving the MDGs. Whilst not eradicated completely, extreme poverty has declined significantly over the last two decades (Figure 1.2). In 1990, nearly half of the population in the developing world lived on less than USD 1.25 a day; that proportion dropped to 14% in 2015 (UNDP, 2015). Life expectancy improved and the global under-five mortality rate declined by more than half, dropping from 90 to 43 deaths per 1,000 births between 1990 and 2015 (Figure 1.3). Productive employment in the developing world expanded massively and unskilled workers saw real increases in their wages. Literacy became more widespread than ever and the primary school net enrolment rate in developing regions increased from 83% in 2000 to 91% in 2015 (UNDP, 2015).

The improved economic performance of developing countries and progress towards the MDGs has stimulated a discussion on what constitutes development in a shifting wealth world. Development is being re-conceptualised as a universal, multi-dimensional process that goes beyond economic growth. Improving the livelihoods and well-being of individuals globally is increasingly viewed as the appropriate objective of development rather than raising GDP. This is demonstrated by the rise in popularity of metrics such as the Better Life Index, the HDI and the Social Progress Index. The recently agreed-upon Sustainable Development Goals (SDGs) embody this multi-dimensional conception and work to further break down the dichotomy between developed and developing countries.

Figure 1.1. **Non-OECD countries' share in the global economy has been rising steadily**

Share of GDP in PPP (current USD)

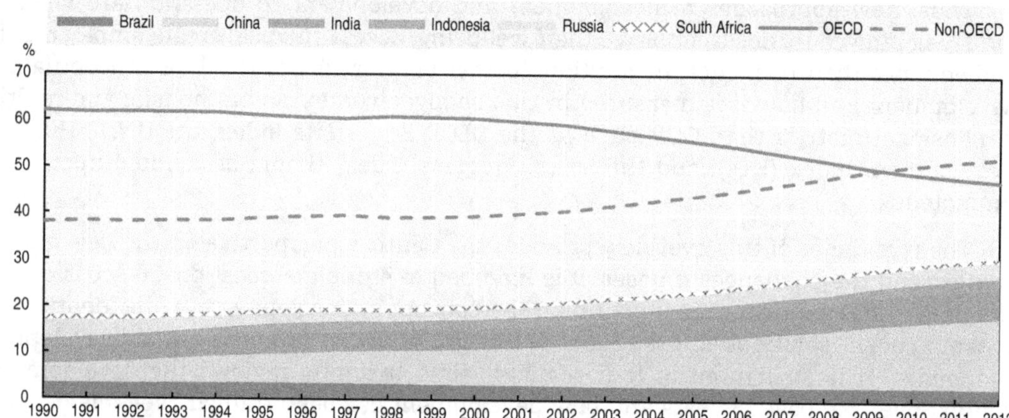

Source: OECD (2014a), *Perspectives on Global Development 2014: Boosting Productivity to Meet the Middle-Income Challenge.*

Figure 1.2. **All developing regions have reduced the share of their populations living in extreme poverty**

Poverty headcount ratio by region, %, 2005 PPPs, 1990-2010

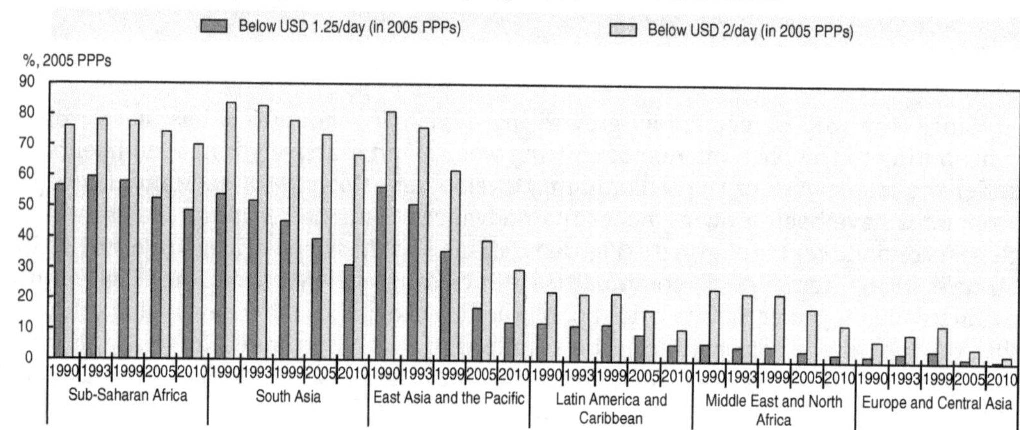

Source: OECD (2015a), *Securing Livelihoods for All: Foresight for Action.*

Figure 1.3. **There has been robust global progress in reducing under-five mortality rates**

Under five mortality rates, 1990 and 2013

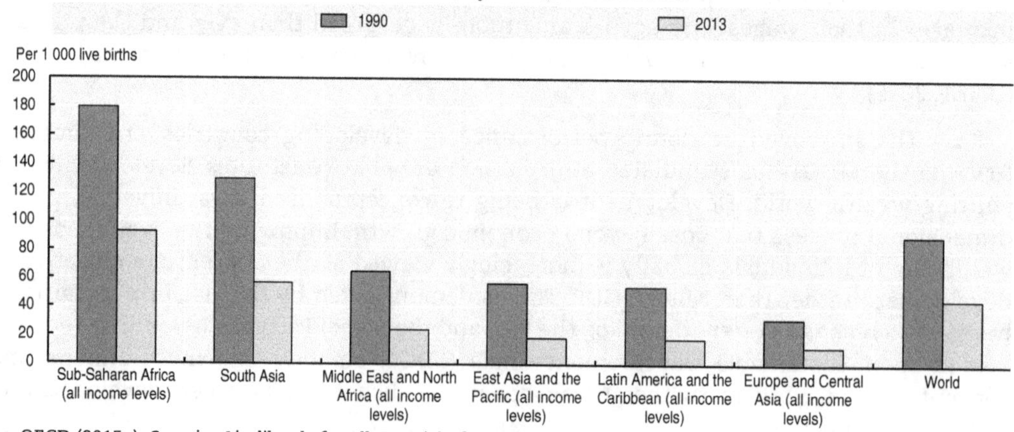

Source: OECD (2015a), *Securing Livelihoods for All: Foresight for Action.*

Is shifting wealth over? A new, more challenging global context

More recently, however, signs suggest that this may have been an exceptional period, and that a new, more challenging global context is emerging. A variety of challenges, including sluggish growth, the end of the commodity super cycle, a more volatile global financial system, demographic transitions and urbanisation, premature deindustrialisation, and environmental shocks, have emerged and will constrain development prospects over the coming 15 years.

Is shifting wealth over?

The global economy is exhibiting perennially sluggish output growth, below target inflation and low interest rates, to the extent that some commentators are heralding the advent of "secular stagnation" (Summers, et al, 2016). Slowing economic convergence between the advanced economies and developing countries potentially heralds the end of the shifting wealth phenomenon of the last 15 years. The growth differential between OECD and non-OECD countries narrowed recently, after its peak in 2009 during the global financial and economic crisis. At current rates (average growth between 2000 and 2012) several lower middle-income countries (e.g. India, Indonesia and Viet Nam) as well as upper middle-income countries (Brazil, Colombia, Hungary, Mexico and South Africa) will fail to catch up with average OECD income levels by 2050 (OECD, 2015a).

Their challenge is deepened by the slowdown in some large developing economies, particularly China (Figure 1.4). After three decades of extraordinary economic development, China is moving towards a lower growth path: growth slowed from a peak of 14% in 2007 to 7.4% in 2014 (OECD, 2015b). This is mainly due to the slowdown in investment and the lagged impact of earlier measures to restrain credit and the housing market boom.

Figure 1.4. **Economic convergence between advanced and emerging economies is slowing down**

GDP growth, 1980-2020

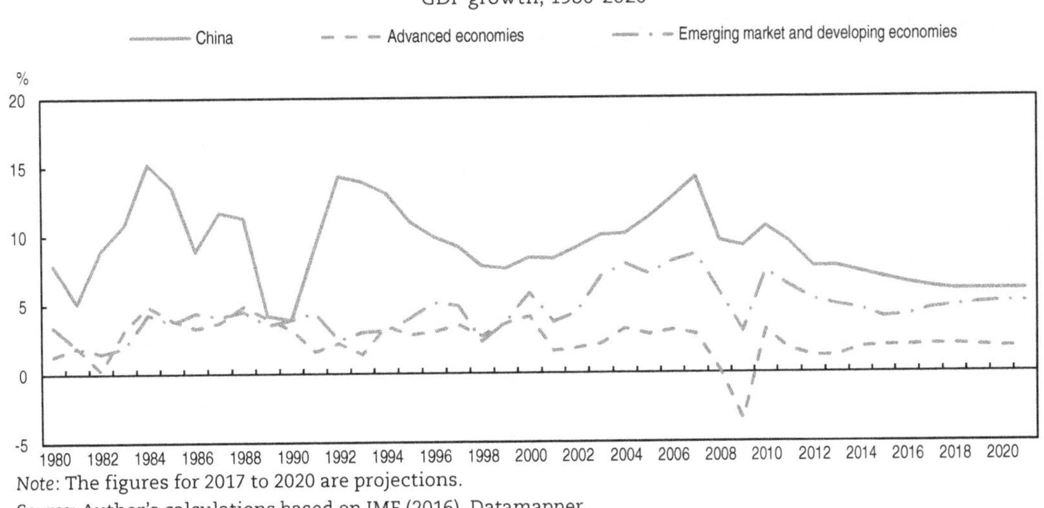

Note: The figures for 2017 to 2020 are projections.

Source: Author's calculations based on IMF (2016), Datamapper.

The commodity super cycle has ended

China is the world's biggest importer of raw materials (Figure 1.5), and as such, its slowdown greatly reduces global demand for raw materials and negatively affects commodity exporters. All commodity price indices, including food, agricultural raw materials, mineral ores and metals, and crude petroleum, declined from 2012 to 2015 (UNCTAD, 2015a). Falling prices were a result of weakening demand, oversupply (following overinvestment during the preceding decade of higher prices), an appreciating dollar and unusually large harvests (World Bank, 2015). Oil prices have been pushed down by decreasing demand from the United States following gains made by fracking and other deposits, and OPEC's decision not to reduce production. The end of the commodity super cycle has been particularly difficult for countries heavily dependent on energy exports: Nigeria and the Plurinational State of Bolivia, for example, suffered large income losses in 2015, ranging from 6% to 12% of GDP, with the Republic of the Congo and South Sudan suffering even larger income declines (IMF, 2015). Pro-cyclical investment strategies pursued by many developing countries have left them vulnerable to price fluctuations. Moreover, the least developed countries (LDCs) are frequently the most dependent on non-renewable natural resources. Almost one quarter of LDCs (11 out of 48) are highly dependent on natural resources rents as an engine of growth and are thus especially susceptible to commodity price shocks (Table 1.1).

Figure 1.5. **China has the largest share of raw material imports**

Raw material imports and China's and India's shares, 2000-12

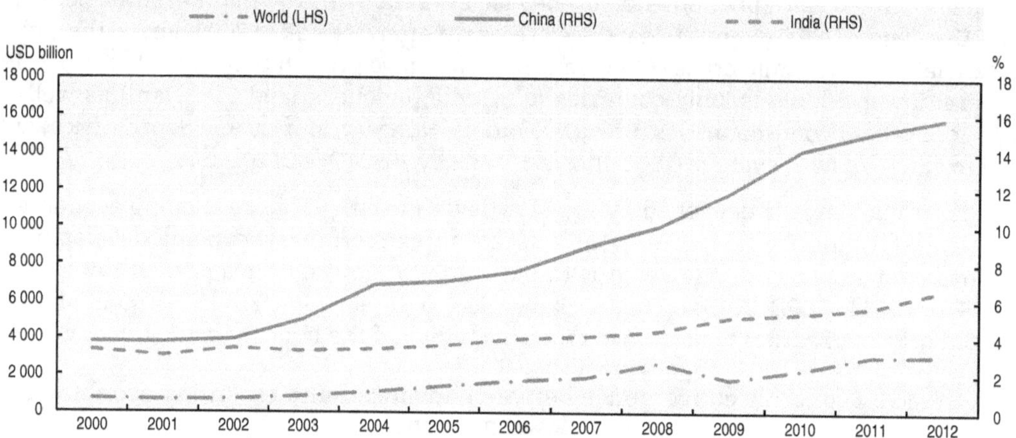

Note: Raw material is defined as the sum of the categories of A, B and C in ISIC Rev.3 where A. is Agriculture, hunting and forestry; B. is Fishing and C. is Mining and quarrying.

Source: OECD (2014a), *Perspectives on Global Development 2014: Boosting Productivity to Meet the Middle-Income Challenge.*

Table 1.1. **LDCs are highly dependent on non-renewable natural resources**

Country	Non-renewable natural resources rents (% of GDP) 2013
Equatorial Guinea	53.3
Mauritania	41.9
Angola	34.6
South Sudan	25.8
Chad	23.3
Democratic Republic of the Congo	21.1
Eritrea	18.8
Zambia	16.6
Yemen	15.7
Burkina Faso	13.7
Lao People's Democratic Republic	10.3

Source: Author's calculations based on World Bank (2016a), World Development Indicators, data.worldbank.org

Access to financial markets is increasingly difficult

The worsening economic climate for developing countries is matched by an increasingly volatile financial system. A combination of a sluggish economy, fiscal austerity and quantitative easing resulted in excess liquidity in developed economies spilling over to emerging economies. Private capital inflows to developing countries, as a proportion of gross national income, increased rapidly from 2.8% in 2002 to 5% in 2013, after reaching a record high of 6.6% in 2007 (UNCTAD, 2015a). However, capital began swiftly exiting developing countries from mid-2015 as global financial markets became concerned with weakening growth in China, recessions in Brazil, the Russian Federation and South Africa, and projected rising interest rates in the United States. These increasingly large and volatile capital flows are reminiscent of the flows that preceded previous financial crises in the 1980s and 1990s. Although they can give a short-term boost to growth, they also can increase vulnerabilities to external shocks.

This volatility is contributing to a difficult financial climate for developing countries. Domestic resource mobilisation remains a significant problem in many emerging economies. Thus, they are more reliant on private capital flows, including portfolio flows and foreign direct investment (FDI), foreign aid, and remittances as a source of finance.

The more constrained global context is making international finance more difficult to come by, however. Portfolio flows are increasingly erratic and speculative, whilst FDI inflows are increasingly concentrated in a few key resource-rich countries: Mozambique, Zambia, Tanzania, Democratic Republic of the Congo, Equatorial Guinea, and Haiti accounted for 58% of total FDI to the LDCs in 2014 (ibid.). Real bilateral official development assistance (ODA) from OECD Development Assistance Committee (DAC) members has stagnated since 2010 (UNCTAD, 2015b). Moreover, over the period until 2030, 28 developing countries with a total population of 2 billion are projected to exceed the income threshold for ODA eligibility (Sedemund, 2014).

Demographic transitions will lead to the rapid expansion of working-age populations in low income regions

These more adverse economic and financial conditions will be exacerbated by large-scale demographic transitions over the next 15 years. Many high and middle-income countries, such as EU member countries and China, will experience population ageing such that their populations will stagnate or begin to decline unless ameliorative policy actions are taken. By contrast, working-age populations will expand rapidly in low-income regions, particularly sub-Saharan Africa and South Asia (Figure 1.6). Africa in particular has experienced a swift decrease in child mortality combined with high fertility rates, contributing to rapid population growth.

Figure 1.6. Working-age populations are expected to grow substantially in low-income regions

Working age population, 1950-2050

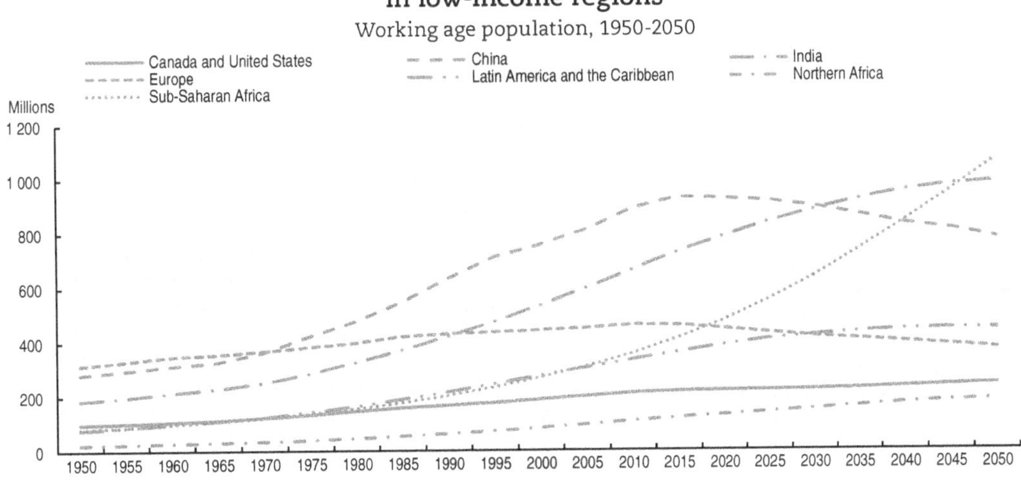

Note: Working-age is defined as 20-64 years old. Figures for 2017-2050 are projections.

Source: UN-DESA (2012a), World Population Prospects: The 2012 Revision.

Creating jobs will be difficult

Countries with large working-age populations can enjoy a "demographic dividend" provided they can create enough jobs. A country's capacity to exploit the demographic dividend relies on its capacity to employ the growing number of young people entering the labour force. Sub-Saharan Africa's labour force is expanding by about 8 million people per year; it will grow by 12 million per year in South Asia (World Bank, 2012). Around 600 million more jobs are needed in 2020 than in 2005 to maintain the world's ratio of employment to working-age population (ibid.). However, the gap between the number of jobs and the working-age population is significant, and is growing in several regions; it may reach about 200 million in sub-Saharan Africa in 2030 (Figure 1.7).

Figure 1.7. The gap is growing between the number of jobs and the working-age population, 1991-2030

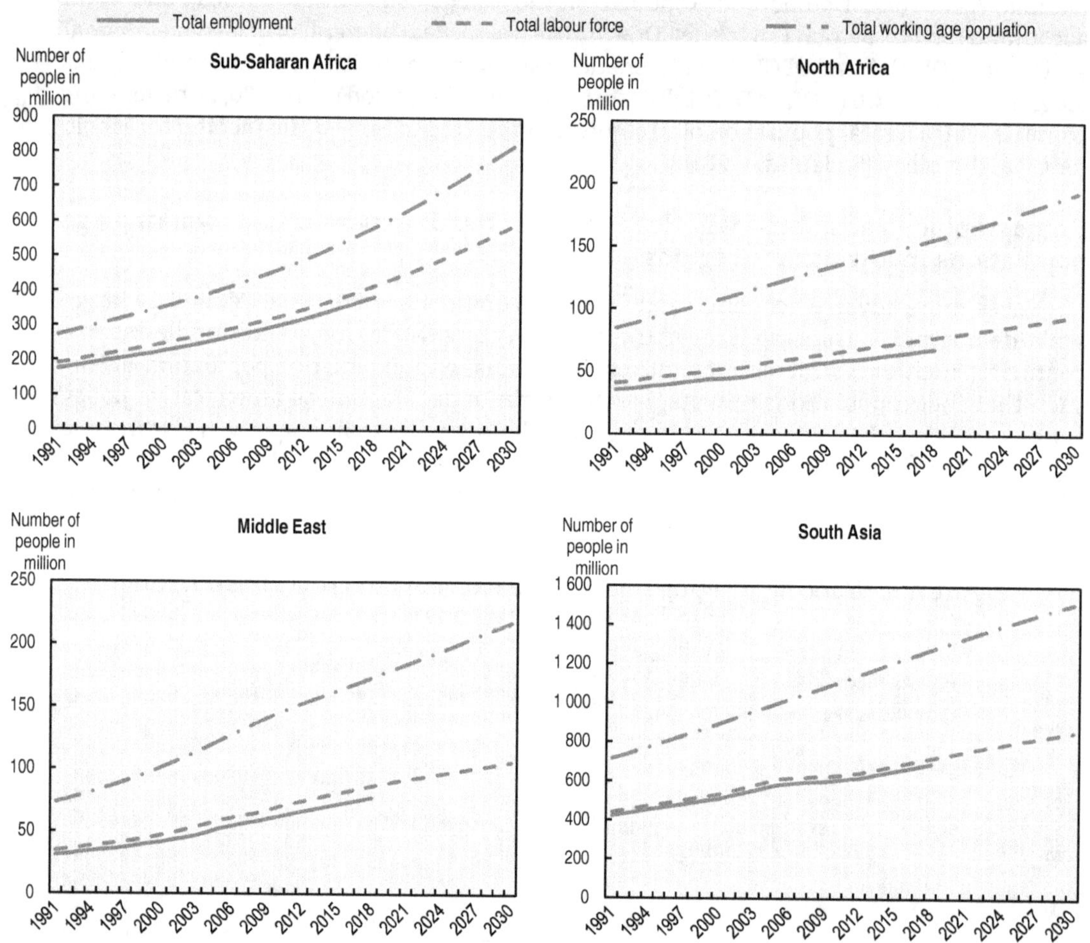

Note: Projections start in 2014. The labour force is the actual number of people available for work. The labour force of a country included both the employed and the unemployed (that is those looking for a job).
Source: OECD (2015a), *Securing Livelihoods for All: Foresight for Action*.

Furthermore, ensuring economic growth itself may not be enough to create jobs. GDP growth and employment growth are decoupling across all countries. This trend has been especially pronounced since the 2000s, reflecting the productivity gains and unemployment problems experienced by a number of countries. Among the BRIICS (Brazil, the Russian Federation, India, Indonesia, China and South Africa), China's case is particularly striking (Figure 1.8): between 1991 and 2012, GDP multiplied by a factor of nine (adjusted for inflation), while total employment remained almost static. Meanwhile, the labour force participation rate diminished by some eight percentage points, from 85% of the 15-64 age group in 1991 to 77% in 2012. The phenomenon is similarly remarkable in India (Figure 1.8), although the labour force participation rate declined less steeply than in China, reflecting the informal economy's greater size. Jobless growth also is occurring in low-income countries such as Bangladesh (Figure 1.9). Rapid population growth in sub-Saharan Africa, in particular, combined with jobless growth, will contribute to growing migration from the South to the North. Global migration is welfare-enhancing overall, in terms of raising labour productivity, generating remittances, and enhancing skill development but there are local winners and losers (OECD, 2016b). Integrating migrants into society is a policy challenge for all countries.

Figure 1.8. **Employment growth is stagnating in China and India**

Indexed GDP (constant 2005 USD), total employment and total labour force, 1991=100 (LHS); labour force participation rate, in % of total population ages 15-64 (RHS)

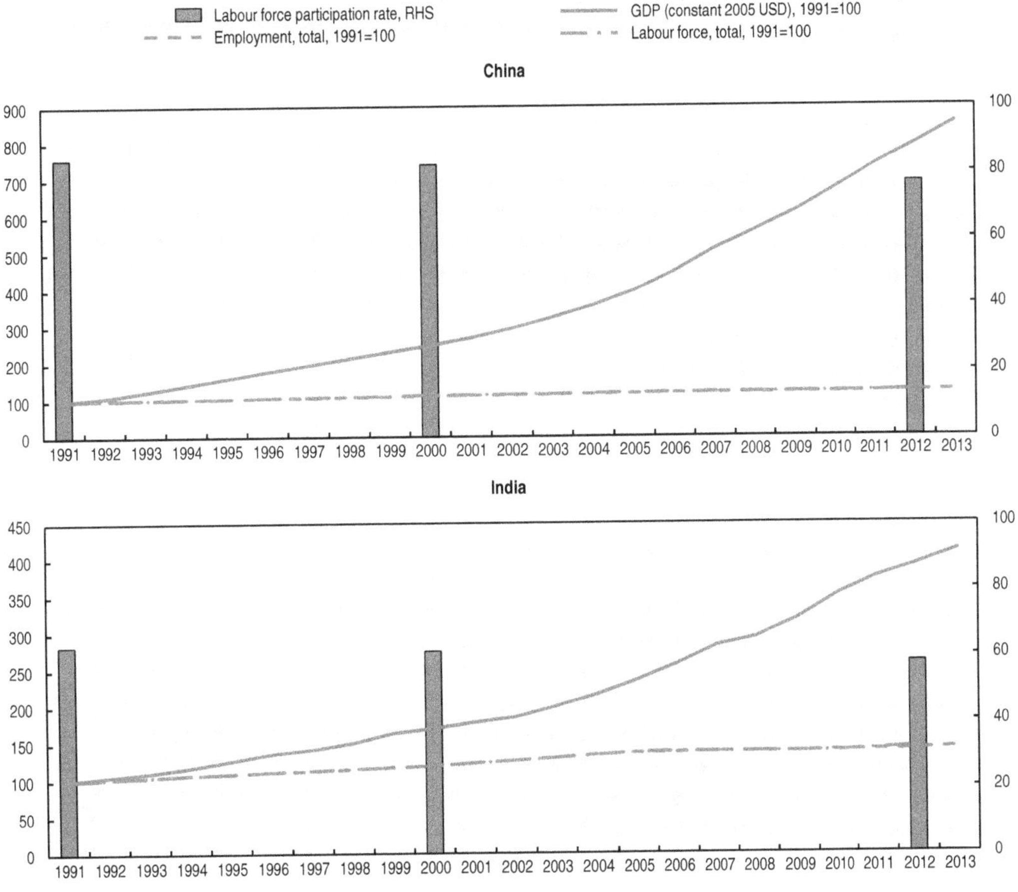

Notes: The labour force is the actual number of people available for work. The labour force of a country includes both the employed and the unemployed (that is those looking for a job). RHS means right-hand side axis. LHS means left-hand side axis.

Source: OECD (2015a), *Securing Livelihoods for All: Foresight for Action.*

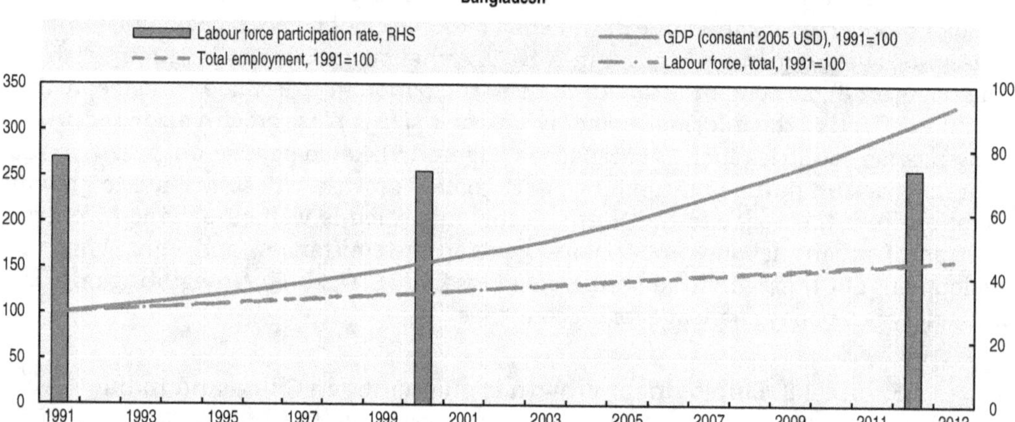

Figure 1.9. Jobless growth is also occurring in low-income countries

Indexed GDP (constant 2005 USD), total employment and total labour force, 1991=100 (LHS); labour force participation rate, in % of total population ages 15-64 (RHS)

Notes: The labour force is the actual number of people available for work. The labour force of a country includes both the employed and the unemployed (that is those looking for a job). RHS means right-hand side axis. LHS means left-hand side axis.

Source: OECD (2015a), *Securing Livelihoods for All: Foresight for Action.*

Digitalisation and automation could accelerate these trends. Enhanced processing power, big data analytics and improved robotics are enabling machines to increasing perform both routine manual and routine cognitive tasks more cheaply and effectively than people. Nike used 106 000 fewer contract workers in 2013 than in 2012 because it is "shifting toward automation," even in lower-margin countries such as China, Indonesia and Viet Nam (McAfee, 2014). The rise of 3D printing and additive manufacturing has the potential to re-localise parts of the production process and shorten global supply chains, with significant implications for jobs in low-value added manufacturing activities in developing countries.

Urbanisation is increasing rapidly in developing regions

Furthermore, these demographic and employment challenges are occurring during a period of rapid urbanisation in developing regions (Figure 1.10). While urban population growth is expected to continue in OECD countries, most of the growth of the world's urban population is projected to occur in non-OECD economies. In Asia, for example, the level of urbanisation is forecasted to increase from 45% in 2011 to 64% in 2050, when about 1.4 billion more people will be living in cities. In comparison, urbanisation in North America will rise by less than 10 percentage points to around 89% in 2050, but will still remain more than 24 percentage points above Asia. These rapid urbanisation trends will present significant challenges in terms of mitigating environmental problems, such as freshwater supplies, waste disposal and air pollution, and managing rising infrastructure costs.

Figure 1.10. **Developing regions are urbanising rapidly**

Level of urbanisation by region, 1960-2050 (projected)

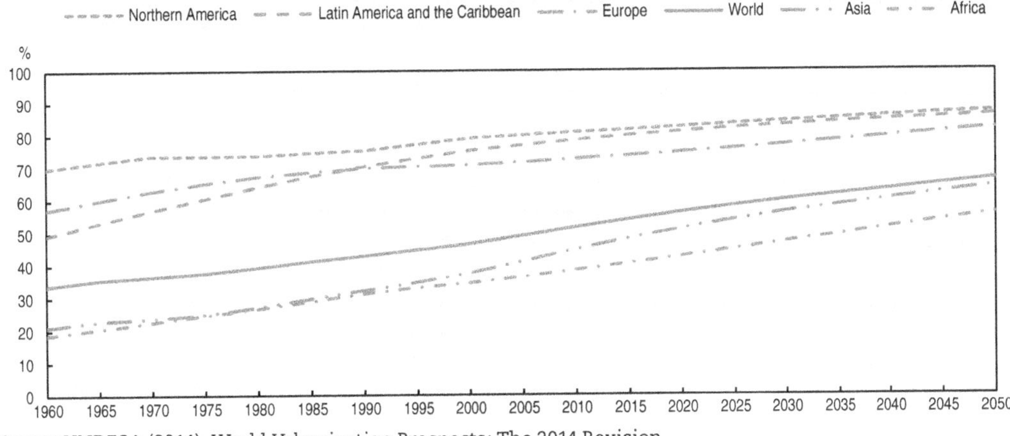

Source: UNDESA (2014), *World Urbanization Prospects: The 2014 Revision.*

Climate change is expected to reduce economic growth in most regions

Tackling these challenges will be exacerbated by climate-related shocks, the burden of which fall disproportionately on developing countries. Environmental degradation and GDP growth are tightly and negatively correlated (van Zanden, 2014) and climate change is expected to reduce economic growth in most regions (Figure 1.11). The International Panel on Climate Change (IPCC) estimates that the global mean temperature will increase by 0.5-1.2 degrees Celsius between 2015 and 2035 (IPCC, 2014). Significant portions of plant and animal species face extinction risks as a result. The frequency of natural hazards, such as floods, droughts, typhoons and hurricanes, is already increasing because of climate change. The number of people exposed to droughts is expected to increase by 9% to 17% in 2030. The number exposed to river floods is expected to increase by 4% to 15% in 2030 (World Bank, 2016). Coastal systems and low-lying areas are at increasing risk from sea level rise, which will continue for centuries even if the global mean temperature is stabilised (IPCC, 2014). As such, low-lying developing countries, such as Bangladesh and the Philippines, face significant humanitarian problems.

Figure 1.11. **Climate change will reduce economic growth in most regions**

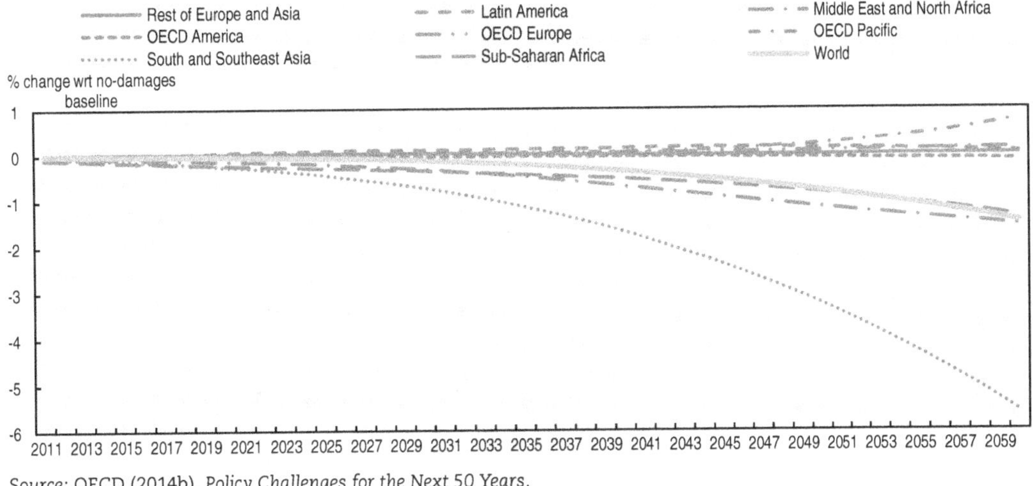

Source: OECD (2014b), *Policy Challenges for the Next 50 Years.*

Climate change poses a significant threat to food security: fisheries productivity and wheat, rice and maize production in tropical regions will be severely challenged. Water scarcity will become increasingly prevalent in light of the projected reduction in renewable surface water and groundwater resources. Climate change also is expected to affect human health by compounding existing health problems and diseases, such as malaria and diarrhoea.

Poorer people suffer disproportionately from climate-related shocks. In the absence of rapid and inclusive development policies, climate change could result in an additional 100 million people, mostly based in developing countries, living in poverty by 2030 (World Bank, 2016b).

Conflict and new forms of security risks are destabilising many states

Peace and security are essential for development but conflict and new forms of security risks are destabilising many states. 1.5 billion people – about one-fifth of the world's population – live in countries affected by conflict. Protracted conflicts predominate in low-income countries and have negative impacts on development, as demonstrated by the rise in poverty in such countries. For example, countries that experienced major violence between 1981 and 2005 had on average a poverty rate 21 percentage points higher than countries that experience no violence (World Bank, 2011). The negative externalities of conflicts spill over to other countries and the burden falls disproportionately on developing countries: 75% of refugees are hosted by neighbouring countries and developing regions hosted 86% of the world's refugees in 2014 (UNHCR, 2015). Global forced displacement has been accelerating, reaching unprecedented levels. By the end of 2014, 59.5 million people were forcibly displaced worldwide as a result of conflict, persecution and human rights violations (ibid.) Moreover, whilst inter-state conflicts have declined, other forms of security risks have become more prominent. Terrorism has become an increasingly salient problem for advanced countries since 9/11, as demonstrated by the recent attacks in Paris and Nice. The rise of rogue terrorist groups, such as Al-Qaeda in the Arabian Peninsula (AQAP) in Yemen, Boko Harem in Nigeria and Al-Shabaab in Somalia, is making governance in already fragile states increasingly precarious. These groups are furthermore propagating conflict and human displacement beyond the borders of their origin countries.

Faced with these challenges, tried and tested development strategies may no longer deliver results. Developing countries have looked historically to manufacturing to absorb significant amounts of unskilled labour and act as growth engines of the future. However, these previously successful industrial-oriented models of development as practiced by China and the East Asian Tigers may no longer work in the new global context. A combination of automation and competitive trade with wealthier countries is contributing to a growing trend of "premature deindustrialisation," whereby developing countries are becoming service economies without experiencing industrialisation (Rodrik, 2015). The problematic consequences of this are already evident. In Latin America, informality has expanded and productivity has dipped as manufacturing as a share of the economy has declined. In Africa, urban and rural migrants are moving into informal services instead of manufacturing despite Chinese investment in industry. The sustainability of growth in these regions is thus questionable as it is propped up by capital inflows, transfers or commodity booms rather than domestic sources.

Development co-operation needs to adapt to the new context

New approaches to development co-operation are therefore required. The realisation that aid alone is insufficient to achieve shared development goals, and the recognition of an evolving and increasingly complex development architecture, characterised by a greater variety of actors, country contexts and new forms of partnership, has driven the impetus for new forms of development co-operation in the 2030 Agenda for Sustainable Development era. Examples of this were already outlined in the 2011 Busan Partnership for Effective Development Co-Operation: strengthen ownership of development priorities by developing countries, focus on results, build inclusive development partnerships, and enhance transparency and accountability (OECD, 2014c). In consultation with the international community, the OECD Development Co-operation Directorate (DCD-DAC) is building on this work through its development of a new statistical measurement to measure "external" finance that supports developing countries. Total official support for sustainable development (TOSSD) covers all officially-supported resource flows regardless of financial instrument used or level of concessionality, or whether they are delivered through bilateral or multilateral channels (OECD, 2016c). TOSSD will promote greater transparency of the full array of external officially-supported resources available to finance the SDGs and to address development enablers and global challenges. Other novel forms of development co-operation beyond measures like TOSSD are required to meet the SDGs.

Perspectives from developing and emerging economies

Sluggish growth, the end of the commodity super cycle, a more volatile global financial system, demographic transitions, migration and urbanisation, premature deindustrialisation, environmental shocks, and conflict and security issues will combine and interact with one another to create a more constrained development context for emerging countries. It is easy to be pessimistic in light of such a gloomy prognosis. However, the next 15 years are also a period of opportunity to enhance the resilience of developing countries.

The contributions in this anthology from a range of thought leaders across the world are testament to the opportunities and positive policy options in the face of such challenges. The remainder of this anthology is split into four chapters. **Chapter 2** analyses some of the major risks and challenges associated with structural transformation in sub-Saharan Africa and Azerbaijan. Common among these pieces is the recognition that development based largely on agricultural and extractive resources is susceptible to commodity price fluctuations and thus unsustainable in the long-term.

- Alan Hirsch recognises many African countries' dependency on natural resources' rents, and the problems this poses in light of falling commodity prices.
- Similarly, using Tanzania to highlight development challenges common to many sub-Saharan African countries, Donald Mmari emphasises the dependency on agriculture and the need to both enhance agricultural productivity and diversify to other higher-value activities.
- Vugar Bayramov and Ahmad Alili, note Azerbaijan's dependency on rents from natural oil and gas reserves to spur its economic growth over the past 15 years. Falling energy prices means this growth model is no longer fit for purpose.
- Neuma Grobbelaar outlines five key game changers for Africa that will help accelerate progress toward the SDGs: managing the impact of climate change and moving away from a carbon intensive growth path; addressing the infrastructure gap and the role of domestic resource mobilisation; tackling the digital divide; accelerating land reform; and using migration as a positive driver of development.

Chapter 3 discusses building inclusive societies in the context of rapid demographic change, jobless growth, rising informality and growing inequality.

- René N'Guettia Kouassi contends that growing inequality between countries is the key development challenge over the coming 15 years. Such inequality perpetuates various problems such as conflicts and the migration crisis. Countries should improve social protection programs to reduce inequality.

- Gilbert Houngbo emphasises the need to create secure jobs for young people on a global scale, citing the disproportional number of young people "working and producing in the informal economy." He calls for incentives for formal job creation, initiatives to formalise informal jobs and units, and the extension of social coverage to informal workers.

- Similarly, Samir Saran and Vivan Sharan stress the high proportion of young Indians in the working-age Indian population without jobs or in informal employment. They argue that recognition of the "new informality" is needed and hope technology could provide for India's informal workforce by identifying informal workers and guaranteeing them some minimum level of income, health and life insurance coverage, and safe and healthy working conditions.

- Hussein Al-Majali notes the problem of youth unemployment and labour market restrictions in the MENA region. He advocates that MENA countries develop the concept of "active citizenship," based on ample employment opportunities, for the disaffected youth of the region.

Chapter 4 explores the risks and challenges associated with reconciling growing energy demands, energy security and the transition to low-carbon economies in the context of the BRICS and ASEAN community.

- Sanjayan Velautham highlights the ASEAN community's challenge of overcoming the "energy trilemma": finding the optimal balance between energy security, environmental sustainability and economic competitiveness as ASEAN is projected to require more than 2.4 times its current annual energy demand over the next 15 years.

- Tian Huifang looks at the competitiveness, institutional, regulatory, infrastructural and financial barriers the BRICS face as they transition to a low-carbon economy in the context of high energy consumption, high emissions and heavy pollution. She calls on G20 countries to renew their commitment to global climate governance by reinforcing the Paris Agreement, pushing developed countries to meet the commitment to mobilise USD 100 billion per year by 2020 to support climate change adaptation and mitigation and foster other sources of climate finance.

Chapter 5 looks at the concept of development cooperation in the context of the LDCs and the SDGs.

- Debapriya Bhattacharya and Sarah Sabin Khan explore the prospect of the LDCs being left behind in the SDGs agenda. They propose three key policy areas on which to focus: increased financial resources and access to technology and support for capacity building from the international community; enhanced protection from various systemic risks; and enabling domestic reforms to complement international support measures.

- Andrea Vignolo and Karen Van Rompaey argue that the eligibility and graduation criteria for ODA rooted in countries' economic growth performance are increasingly outdated within the SDGs agenda that sees development as a multi-dimensional process based on well-being and sustainability rather than just GDP growth. Continuing to develop other forms of development co-operation, such as South-South and triangular co-operation, will thus be increasingly important.

References

IMF (2016), *Datamapper*, http://www.imf.org/external/datamapper/index.php?db=FM

IMF (2015), *Macroeconomic Developments and Prospects in Low-Income Developing Countries: 2015*, International Monetary Fund, Washington, DC, https://www.imf.org/external/np/pp/eng/2015/111915.pdf

IPCC (2014), *Climate Change 2014: Synthesis Report.* Contribution of Working Groups I, II and III to the Fifth Assessment Report of the Intergovernmental Panel on Climate Change [Core Writing Team, R.K. Pachauri and L.A. Meyer (eds.)]. Intergovernmental Panel on Climate Change, Geneva, Switzerland.

McAfee, M. (2014) "Even Sweatshops are Getting Automated. So What's Left?" Andrew McAfee, May 2014. http://andrewmcafee.org/2014/05/mcafee-nike-automation-labor-technology-globalization/.

OECD (2016a), "The untold Shifting Wealth story: remaining vulnerabilities", issues paper prepared for OECD Development Centre inaugural meeting on Development in Transition, 13 December 2016.

OECD (2016b), *Perspectives on Global Development 2017: International Migration,* OECD Publishing, Paris, http://dx.doi.org/10.1787/persp_glob_dev-2017-en.

OECD (2016c), *TOSSD Compendium,* OECD Publishing, Paris, http://www.oecd.org/dac/financing-sustainable-development/TOSSD%20Compendium2016.pdf.

OECD (2015a), *Securing Livelihoods for All: Foresight for Action,* Development Centre Studies, OECD Publishing, Paris, http://dx.doi.org/10.1787/9789264231894-en.

OECD (2015b), *Economic Surveys China,* OECD Publishing, Paris, http://dx.doi.org/10.1787/eco_surveys-chn-2015-en.

OECD (2014a), *Perspectives on Global Development 2014: Boosting Productivity to Meet the Middle-Income Challenge,* OECD Publishing, Paris, http://dx.doi.org/10.1787/persp_glob_dev-2014-en.

OECD (2014b) *Policy Challenges for the Next 50 Years,* Economic Policy Paper, OECD Publishing, Paris, http://dx.doi.org/10.1787/5jz18gs5fckf-en.

OECD/UNDP (2014c), *Making Development Co-operation More Effective: 2014 Progress Report,* OECD Publishing, Paris, http://dx.doi.org/10.1787/9789264209305-en.

OECD (2013), *OECD Guidelines on Measuring Subjective Well-being,* OECD Publishing, Paris, http://dx.doi.org/10.1787/9789264191655-en.

Rodrik, D., "Premature Deindustrialisation ", *NBER Working Paper* No. 20935, February 2015.

Sedemund, J. (2014), "An outlook on ODA graduation in the post-2015 era", External Financing for Development, OECD Publishing, Paris, http://www.oecd.org/dac/financing-sustainable-development/ERG%20S2%20Jan%202014%20-%20Does%20Aid%20Have%20a%20Future%20-%20Serge%20Tomasi%202014%2001.pdf.

Summers, L. H., et al (2016), "Secular Stagnation in the Open Economy", *NBER Working Paper* No. 22172, April.

Tregenna, F. (2015), "Deindustrialisation, structural change and sustainable economic growth", *Inclusive and Sustainable Industrial Development Working Paper Series,* WP 02, United Nations Industrial Development Organization, http://www.unido.org//fileadmin/user_media/Services/PSD/WP_2015_02_v2.pdf.

UNCTAD (2015a), *The Least Developed Countries Report 2015: Transforming Rural Economies,* United Nations publications, New York and Geneva, http://unctad.org/en/PublicationsLibrary/ldc2015_en.pdf.

UNCTAD (2015b), *Trade and Development Report 2015: Making the international financial architecture work for development,* United Nations publications, New York and Geneva, http://unctad.org/en/PublicationsLibrary/tdr2015_en.pdf.

UNDP (2015), *The Millennium Development Goals Report 2015,* United Nations publications, New York and Geneva, http://www.un.org/millenniumgoals/2015_MDG_Report/pdf/MDG%202015%20rev%20(July%201).pdf.

UNHCR (2015), *World at War. Forced Displacement in 2014,* United Nations publications, New York and Geneva, http://www.unhcr.org/556725e69.pdf.

Van Zanden, J., et al. (eds.) (2014), How was Life? Global Well-Being Since 1820, OECD Publishing, Paris, 10.1787/9789264214262-en.

WEF (2016), *The Global Risks Report 2016,* World Economic Forum, Geneva, http://www3.weforum.org/docs/Media/TheGlobalRisksReport2016.pdf.

World Bank (2016a), *World Development Indicators* (database), data.worldbank.org/indicator.

World Bank (2016b), *Shockwaves. Managing the Impacts of Climate Change on Poverty*, The World Bank Group, Washington, DC., https://openknowledge.worldbank.org/bitstream/handle/10986/22787/9781464806735.pdf.

World Bank (2015), *Commodity Markets Outlook (April)*, The World Bank Group, Washington, DC., http://documents.worldbank.org/curated/en/452351468172786553/pdf/96001-WP-PUBLIC-Box391432B-ADD-SERIES-GEP2015b-commodity-Apr2015-PUBLIC.pdf.

World Bank (2012), *World Development Report 2013: Jobs*, The World Bank Group, Washington, DC., https://siteresources.worldbank.org/EXTNWDR2013/Resources/8258024-1320950747192/8260293-1322665883147/WDR_2013_Report.pdf.

World Bank (2011), *World Development Report 2011: Conflict, Security and Development*, The World Bank Group, Washington, DC., http://siteresources.worldbank.org/INTWDRS/Resources/WDR2011_Full_Text.pdf.

Chapter 2

Structural transformation in a changing development context

Chapter 2 deals with the topic of structural transformation in a new macro environment. The previous 15 years were favourable toward developing and emerging economies, partly because of strong growth in China and a commodity price boom. It is uncertain whether these conditions will prevail over the next 15 years and development strategies based on agriculture and extractive industries may no longer be sustainable. Alan Hirsch writes about the growth take-off in Africa during the 1990s and 2000s and that although there are many obstacles to African development, there are reasons to be hopeful. Donald Mmari draws on the experience of Tanzania to offer policy advice on diversification for sub-Saharan Africa. Neuma Grobbelaar outlines five "game changers" that have the potential to accelerate African development if harnessed correctly. Vugar Bayramov and Ahmad Alili put forward a vision for a prosperous Azerbaijan not dependent on oil and gas reserves.

The period of shifting wealth may be coming to an end. As identified in the preceding overview, the global economy is exhibiting sluggish output growth, below target inflation and low interest rates. This is caused partly by the slowdown in some large emerging economies, particularly the People's Republic of China (hereafter, China). As the world's largest importer of raw materials, China's slowdown greatly reduces the demand for raw materials – the resulting end of the commodity super cycle has significant implications for developing countries heavily reliant on natural resources' rents. The worsening economic climate is also contributing to an increasingly volatile global financial system, which many developing countries are finding difficult to access. Furthermore, digitalisation and automation have the potential to accelerate the trend of premature deindustrialisation: manufacturing as a share of total employment has stagnated or fallen in all developing regions except South Asia since 1990. In this new context, previously successful development strategies based on commodity exports or industrialisation may no longer be sustainable.

The authors of the sections in this Chapter explore some of these risks and challenges in the contexts of sub-Saharan Africa and Azerbaijan. One risk examined by several of the authors is the over-reliance on certain sectors within the economy. Donald Mmari uses the case of Tanzania to illustrate a problem common to many sub-Saharan African countries: the majority of Tanzanians derive their livelihoods from agriculture, which is based on low-productivity smallholder farms.

Alan Hirsch recognises the key role played by the commodity super cycle and China's large-scale infrastructure investments in Africa's growth take-off during the mid-1990s and 2000s. Because of rising commodity prices and China's investment drive, many sub-Saharan African countries became more dependent on extractive industries during this period. In a similar vein, Vugar Bayramov and Ahmad Alili highlight Azerbaijan's reliance on large oil and gas reserves and rising commodity prices during the past 15 years.

The challenge of diversification thus emerges from all these sections. Diversification will be difficult, however, because Tanzania and other sub-Saharan African countries do not possess the requisite levels of technological readiness, skilled workers and infrastructure to move to higher-productivity activities, including manufacturing. Whilst more advanced along these indices, Azerbaijan faces similar problems. Moreover, the twin "economic policy risks" – as Hirsch calls them – of high levels of inequality and large capital account and fiscal deficits could severely impede development in sub-Saharan Africa if mismanaged.

Positive trends exist. Neuma Grobbelaar identifies five "game changers" that have the potential to invigorate Africa's growth and development, including mobilising domestic resources to address the infrastructure gap, accelerating land reform and using migration as a positive driver of development. Hirsch is similarly optimistic about the growth of SMEs in many parts of Africa, the recent surge in infrastructure investment, and regional success stories, such as East Africa, which is exhibiting improved trade integration, freer movement of people and enhanced cross-border banking. Bayramov and Alili also contend that further integration with regional trading blocs, such as the EU Eastern Partnership programme and international institutions, such as the WTO, will place Azerbaijan on a positive development trajectory.

Taken together, the contributors to this Chapter underscore some of the key risks and challenges of structural transformation facing emerging economies and provide some policy measures for overcoming them. The contributions to this Chapter neither represent the positions of the Development Centre nor the OECD, but are solely the authors' own views.

Section 1. Risks and challenges to sustainable growth and development in Africa
Alan Hirsch[1]

As we know, growth accelerations are pretty commonplace among developing countries. There were 83 growth accelerations of eight consecutive years at 2% higher than the five-yearly average between the mid-1950s and early 2000s (Hausmann, Pritchett and Rodrik, 2005). But most growth accelerations, and especially those in Africa, were short-lived and did not form the foundation of a long-term step-change to a more diversified growth path. Drawing on the language of W.W. Rostow, most growth accelerations do not amount to a "take-off".

The risk following the recently ended booms is that due to insufficient planning and excessive optimism the windfalls of the most recent round of growth accelerations were wasted.

Have the growth accelerations completely fizzled out or has the slowdown in recent years left developmental legacies that can be built upon? Or, have some African countries used the opportunities in recent decades to implement effective longer term growth and development strategies?

Since the early 1990s many African countries have been on a trajectory of higher growth. The global financial crisis in 2007-9, to the surprise of many observers, did not spell the end of Africa's growth surge, though the rate of growth moderated somewhat (Figure 2.1). More recently African growth has slowed further and, at around 4% in GDP terms, it is considerably lower than the 6% plus for emerging Asia. Yet growth remains stronger than in the "lost decades" between the mid-1970s and mid-1990s. In some countries, particularly but not only those less dependent on a narrow range of commodity exports, a higher rate of growth has been maintained.

Figure 2.1. **Growth in sub-Saharan Africa moderated somewhat after the global financial crisis**

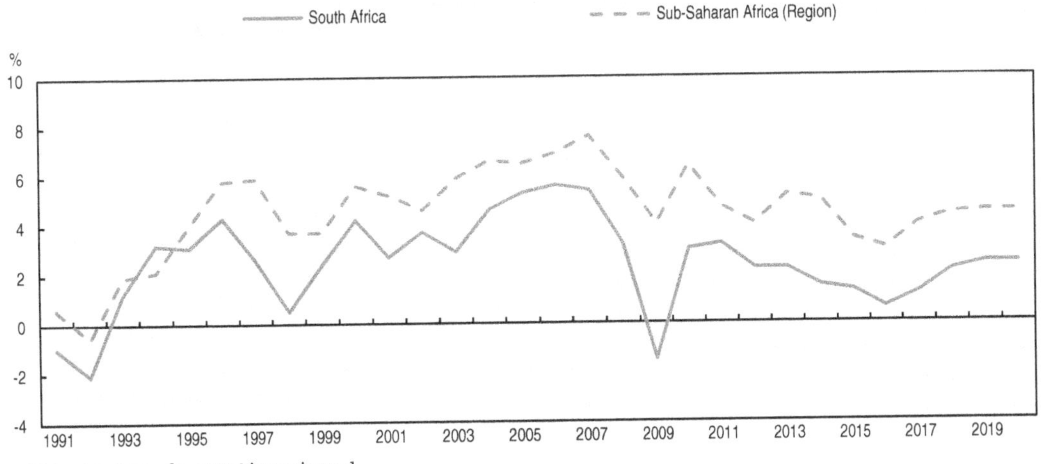

Note: All data after 2016 is projected.

Source: Author's calculations based on IMF (2016), Datamapper.

Africa's developmental performance has improved considerably since the early 1990s. It is evident that African poverty and infant mortality, while still lagging, has improved significantly in recent decades (see Figures 1.2 and 1.3 of the overview chapter). Data would show similar improvements in education access and in access to infrastructural services such as roads and electricity. The higher rate of growth has been a valuable asset, though it is by no means the only factor which has allowed developmental improvements. While these developmental improvements have themselves contributed to growth, the current relatively low growth rate inhibits the pace of the improvement in the lives of Africans.

As Amadou Sy (2016) points out, the current expected pace of per capita growth, in an environment of rapidly growing populations, would lead to a very slow rate of improvement in per capital income and the capacity of African countries to improve the lives of citizens, compared with the pace of growth in the first decade of the 21st century. "If the region was able to regain its 2004-2014 growth rate" argues Sy, "GDP per capita could be doubled in 20.5 years, by 2036. In contrast, at a [per capita] growth rate of 1.4% as currently predicted, this achievement would only be realised in 50 years, by the year 2065."

Growth factors

To get a real sense of why growth has slowed (reducing the capacity for rapid development), we first need to ask why the period since the mid-1990s was so much better than the previous two decades.

The commodity super cycle, centred on China's huge public and private investments, was the standout economic factor in recent decades for Africa through the demand for African products (see Figure 1.5). Later, China's capital surplus due to its export-based growth allowed it to offer huge credits for infrastructure investments in Africa as Chinese infrastructure growth began to wind down.

But indicators show that growth and development improvements began in Africa before the super cycle. While the commodity supercycle underwrote many of Africa's accelerations, other factors were at play.

Clearly important was the completion of Africa's liberation—the democratic transitions in Southern Africa. South Africa's post-democratic growth has had a significant impact on the rest of sub-Saharan Africa mostly through outward investment by South Africa's multinationals, but also through rising trade (Arora and Vamvakidis, 2005).

The South Africa factor is a subset of the positive impact of the end of the Cold War which contributed by allowing greater domestic accountability and improved governance in many African countries, not only South Africa and Namibia.

The improvements in governance, encouraged in part by debt relief initiatives (the Heavily Indebted Poor Countries initiative and the Multilateral Debt Relief Initiative) and the Millennium Development Goals programme, in turn created of an environment that frequently encouraged direct and indirect investment.

Reasons for slowdown

African growth slowed after the global crisis, but the slowdown was not as rapid as initially feared, partly because of global mitigation measures (e.g. for trade credits liquidity) and partly because African growth was also driven by rising domestic consumption (including government services) and investment (including infrastructural investment). Growth has slowed down more in recent years in most African countries under the shadow of several economic policy risks.

By economic policy risks, I mean risks which can be lessened or deepened, depending on the quality of economic policy.

Economic policy risks

Even after the global economic crisis, several African countries were able to embark on sovereign bond issues for the first time.

"Before 2006, only South Africa had issued a sovereign bond in sub-Saharan Africa. Since 2009, 14 other countries have issued a total of USD 17 billion in sovereign bonds. These include Angola, the Democratic Republic of the Congo, Côte d'Ivoire, Gabon, Ghana, Kenya, Namibia, Nigeria, Rwanda, Seychelles, Senegal and Tanzania. Excluding South Africa, sub-Saharan sovereigns issued USD 6.3 billion of foreign-currency denominated bonds in 2014 alone." (Nalishebo and Halwampa, 2015).

The bonds were generally issued in foreign currencies (except in South Africa) on expectations of receipts from the continued export of commodities. In several of these countries, faced with lower than expected tax revenues as commodity prices fell, bond finance was used for current expenditure rather than capital investments. Infrastructure spending continued, sometimes funded by concessional loans from China. It is arguable that by 2014 investors should have been wary of high-yield sovereign bond sales. Two years later the IMF is much busier than it has been in Africa since the height of the HIPC programme, and has called for a "policy reset" in Africa.

The impact of twin deficits – fiscal and the capital account of the balance of payments – is potentially greater than simply a sharp and temporary slowdown. Since the early 1990s, democratic governments in Africa have derived some of their legitimacy from slowly but steadily improving living conditions. Cut-backs potentially threaten the legitimacy of open democracies. The Zambian government delayed entering into negotiations for relief from the IMF until after recent elections. If the inevitable debt restructurings are not carefully designed there are potential risks to political stability.

The second major economic policy risk is that growth is tempered with high levels of inequality. High inequality reduces the impact of growth on poverty, and growing inequality is slow to reverse (Bhorat 2016). Africa has the highest Gini co-efficient among continents and in the richer countries of Central and Southern Africa the Gini coefficient is over 0.55. If these inequality levels cannot be reduced, the sustainability of growth in the region will be compromised.

Finally, is it feasible that Africa will meet, let alone beat, target 9.23 of the Sustainable Development Goals, doubling the share of employment and output attributable to the industrial sector? Much of the increase in employment and value added in recent decades has come from the services sector – now over 50% of value added (Page, 2016).

In a study of 72 developing countries spanning 1996 to 2012, the UNU-Wider project on extractives found that 66 (or 88%) had become more dependent on extractives during the commodity super cycle (Roe and Dodd, 2016).

Developing a manufacturing sector requires managerial competence, sufficiently skilled workers, and a good or improving infrastructural environment. It also needs consistent policies and a state that understands and supports industrialisation in order to replicate what Page (2016) calls Asia's export push policies.

Not many African countries meet these criteria currently—the countries seriously striving for recognition as the exceptions are Mauritius (already there) and Ethiopia (Narreinen, 2013; Oqubay, 2015).

Positive trends

But there are significant positive trends in the rest of Africa too, to counteract the growing pessimism about the fate of Africa's recent growth accelerations. These trends could underpin a long term growth and development trajectory.

- Agricultural productivity is rising, not rapidly, but significantly and consistently, including the smallholder sector in many countries.
- Small businesses are proliferating and thriving in many parts of Africa.
- Several African countries, beyond Ethiopia and Mauritius, are committed to industrial or sectoral strategies, and some are being encouraged by development agencies.
- The recent surge of investment in infrastructure, from rural roads to airports, if well managed, offers advantages for producers and traders.
- East Africa is in many ways showing the way forward with better government-business relations (far from perfect), better trade integration, advances in the freedom of movement of people, and in the development of a regional payments system allowing of easier cross-border banking, for example.
- Improvements in health and education access have impacted, and will impact further when quality improves further.
- Finally, African countries have responded to emerging fiscal squeezes with less resistance and denialism, and more resolve, than in the 1980s.

The risks have grown in recent years, but the developmental improvements of the past two decades may well have generated a sufficient legacy to enable many African countries to move to a stronger footing.

Section 2. Transforming sub-Saharan Africa towards modern, industrial-led economies: Challenges and options
Donald Mmari[2]

As the OECD Development Centre correctly observes, the prospects for development in emerging and developing economies are vast, yet confronted by formidable challenges. The past fifteen years have witnessed rapid economic growth and social progress in Asia, led by China and India. Other countries such as Malaysia and Viet Nam have recorded dramatic growth and economic transformation, coupled with increased productivity, visible structural change, and significant poverty reductions. In sub-Saharan Africa, a few countries have also sustained high growth momentum, albeit with different outcomes in social development. Botswana, for example, has achieved upper-middle income status, although its limited economic diversification makes it vulnerable to commodity price shocks. Ethiopia, Tanzania and Rwanda are heralded as among the fastest growing countries in sub-Saharan Africa. Despite such success stories, many challenges remain unresolved. These challenges include slow structural transformation, coupled with increased informality and "premature" deindustrialisation; changing demographics without corresponding investments in key enablers such as skills development, technology and innovation; and an infrastructure gap. Unless addressed in the near future, these shortfalls will reverse the gains from economic growth and frustrate the achievements of development visions in developing countries, resulting in sustained concentration of wealth in developed countries and widened inequality.

Understanding that developing countries are not homogenous, many of those in sub-Saharan Africa share certain traits, on which this article seeks to focus, drawing more from the experience of Tanzania. First, a large majority of their population lives in rural areas and is dependent on agriculture and related livelihoods. Second, industrial development has been slow, if not reversed in terms of the share of manufacturing value added and manufacturing employment. Third, they are dominated by the growing informal sectors, mostly in low productivity trade and services.

Agriculture and rural transformation

A major concern is that the majority of the people of Tanzania derive their livelihood from agriculture, including crops, livestock and fisheries. The latest labour force survey estimates that 67% of the labour force is engaged in agriculture (Tanzania National Bureau of Statistics, 2014). However, past economic growth has not benefited agricultural producers due to generalised low productivity, market-related constraints, limited and high cost finance, and poor skills that undermine innovation and the uptake of new technologies.

Actions are needed to transform agriculture through a holistic approach to agribusiness development and transforming the rural economy into high productivity economic activities. For the great potential that Tanzania has in agriculture, including arable land and a young population, investments must be made to, first, improve farm level productivity. This requires the following interventions:

- Scale up the adoption of improved farming practices, technology and innovation through agricultural research and extension services, these to be complemented by strategic vocational and adult education
- Invest in rural infrastructure, especially roads (and railway linkages), electricity and small scale and community level irrigation
- Promote access to rural finance, particularly in the form of long-term and low cost agriculture development finance

Second, strengthen agricultural markets, making them efficient and accessible to smallholders who constitute the majority of rural producers in most of sub-Saharan Africa. The following interventions are proposed:

- Where large scale commercial farms exists or are being developed, promote linkages between them and small farms in integrated agricultural production systems that include backward linkages to production and supply of inputs and forward linkages to agro-processing, packaging and marketing
- Foster market linkages and invest in affordable storage and processing facilities to minimise post-harvest losses
- Promote effective producer and market organisations to maximise the benefits of both vertical and horizontal co-ordination, including economies of scale, knowledge spillovers, and bargaining power

Third, create opportunities for diversification of the rural economy. While raising productivity and transforming agriculture, governments should create opportunities for the rural population to improve their livelihoods in non-farm activities in rural areas. This entails diversification of the rural economy by promoting value addition and commercial activities, treating agriculture as an important driver in the diversification process. Enterprise development must be supported to facilitate diversification and moving up the value chains through agro-industry services and trade services. This requires the following interventions:

- Public and private investments in agro-processing facilities
- Providing business and technical training to the rural based youth

- Integrating special financing and incentives for rural based enterprises
- Scaling up job-creating public works in rural infrastructure development.

Industrialisation drive in the error of "premature" deindustrialisation

Structural transformation and economic diversification have proved to be necessary for any economy to promote its growth and to build resilience to shocks. At the core of this transformation, as theory suggests, is a movement from low productivity primary production to the more productive and modern manufacturing sector, and later towards service oriented activities. Underlying this transformation is science, technology and innovation that lead to increased productivity in agriculture, which supplies cheap raw materials and surplus labour to industry. The levels of technology and application of science for production and innovation in developing countries is still generally low. According to the *Global Competitiveness Report 2015-16* (WEF, 2015), Tanzania and other sub-Saharan African countries ranked very low in technological readiness and innovation indices, in contrast to the Southeast Asian tigers. This means that the structural change and decline in agriculture in GDP is not necessarily driven by a notable increase in productivity. Other factors, such as diversification towards informal non-farm activities; migration of young people to cities and peri-urban areas; and growth of basic manufacturing, construction, and related service industries explains the change.

For effective and sustainable structural transformation, industrialisation as a fundamental pillar for adding value to primary products, creating the knowledge base for further transformation into knowledge intensive sectors and for creating jobs cannot be avoided. Thus, the following policy initiatives are proposed to promote rapid industrialisation. First, promote resource-based industrialisation, and second support technology and innovation. In this respect, some form of industrial policy will be required to facilitate the transformation of comparative advantages in natural resource-based industries into competitive advantages.

The proposed strategic interventions are:

- Put high priorities in terms of budgets and policy incentives to agro-industry and value addition to primary production and natural resources. Areas with good natural comparative advantages can easily create significant competitive advantages when processed and converted into industrial goods:
  - Agricultural related value addition
    - Sugar cane: ideal soil and climate.
    - Livestock: the sector can form the basis of a leather industry with multiple export opportunities and export of cut and processed meat.
    - Horticulture: land availability, good climatic conditions, regional and international links to export of packed vegetables and fruits.
    - Fruit and nut processing: untapped potential, with less than 10% produce currently processed.
- Mineral and metal-based industries
  - Tanzania has large quantities of iron ore with an estimated reserve base of two billion tonnes and an extractive capacity of 1.25 million tonnes of steel. This can be used to set up a local steel industry with the potential to support Tanzanian industrialisation in the medium to long term. Regional markets in Eastern and Southern Africa provide further impetus to warrant such investments.
  - Natural gas based industries: in addition to its uses as a source of energy and fuel, natural gas can potentially be used as a productive input in a number of

industries i.e. petro-chemicals and fertiliser industries. These are important industries for building the technology base and fostering linkages with other sectors such as agriculture, construction and transport.

- Accumulate and concentrate industrial firms through cluster development, supported by Special Economic Zones (SEZ)
- Adopt trade policy management which is supportive to industrialisation, permitting industry to progressively mature into competitive industry (selective and strategic protection, while ensuring that import cartels are not allowed to threaten the survival of the nascent manufacturing sector)
- Public investment to close the infrastructure gap
- Public investment to promote the education and skills that is relevant for providing the critical mass of semi-skilled and skilled workforce in strategic industries.

Transforming the informal economy

The labour force in most African economies has continued to grow, but structural transformation has not paved the way for the formal sector to create employment for the growing labour force. A recent UNECA-AUC report has shown that the effects of global financial and economic crisis retarded African economic growth and also raised the numbers of the unemployed and poverty rates (UNECA-AUC, 2010). This situation has led to the increasing importance of informal economic activities as a source for employment opportunities and earnings. Data from a number of sub-Saharan African countries show that growth in employment opportunities has been concentrated in the non-wage sector, with the most important source of growth being in the non-farm self-employment sector. Over two thirds of the labour force is employed in the low-productivity informal economy in vulnerable employment (Ibid).

Thus, to reduce the levels of poverty and vulnerability, interventions to increase productivity and earnings in the informal enterprises are essential for accelerating productivity. The proposed interventions are:

- Design and implement policies and supportive measures to raise the level of productivity in informal enterprises by enhancing their access to resources and markets, and legal identity and rights. These include:
  - Enhance the business environment to remove biases of existing policies against informal enterprises, including: macro policies that create demand for the goods and services produced by informal enterprises and workers. For example, requirements for the government Procurement Act set a threshold on the types of goods and services that can only be supplied by micro and small enterprises.
  - Legal recognition of the informal enterprises with a view to realising the empowerment of the owners to access government contracts and supplies, access to services, and access enforcement of property rights
- Design and implement measures to reduce risk, cost of doing business and eliminating institutional biases that work against informal enterprises. These are meant to drive the transition towards formalisation of the informal economy by supporting to organisational development and reform of the legal and regulatory framework that facilitates and simplifies registration and taxation. These include:
  - Promoting access to information and skills development - small informal enterprises need information on markets, technology and business skills, which can be provided more efficiently by public institutions, or market based institutions supported by state

- Strengthening voice and organisation of informal enterprises - most activities in the informal sector are family business and sometimes seen as means for supplementing income or a survival strategy for the urban dwellers who cannot find jobs in the formal sector. Labour contracts are often implicit with no legal standing, and collective bargaining is also hard to implement. Thus there is need to create institutions that can reach this sector effectively and organise them to be more productive and responsive to the technology-induced transformation and growth.

- Appropriate and responsive political governance and development management. Relevant public institutions must reach out to these informal businesses, to better understand their diversity and challenges (including land, finance, knowhow, etc.) and provide solutions to enable them to participate more effectively in the growth and development process.

Section 3. Five game changers for Africa
Neuma Grobbelaar[3]

The overview chapter "Development prospects in a new global context" makes a number of important observations regarding the new paradigm facing development actors. The constraints facing developing countries that seek to pursue the traditional development path, i.e. related to export-orientated industrialisation and the more difficult external environment for especially commodity-dependent economies are well-considered. However, some of the assertions regarding the end of the commodity super cycle, shifting wealth and premature de-industrialisation seem overstated – particularly in a developing world context. More importantly, the anticipated demographic transition that is sketched in the context of Africa and other developing countries seems too linear, not taking into account how urbanisation and growing middle class affluence influence fertility rates. Migration, while currently a major political topic because of the flood of Syrian migrants into Europe as an outcome of war and conflict, is a prominent feature of a globalised world with mobility directly linked to scarce skills sets and economic opportunity. There is no doubt that developing countries face a more challenging global context, but this also presents an opportunity for innovation, rethinking of traditional solutions and experimentation. It is also important to note that a focus on getting the basics right is critical in creating an enabling environment for development, i.e. pursuing policies that create regulatory certainty and consistency, that enable the private sector to flourish within proper checks and balances, that respect planetary boundaries and global commitments to combating climate change and that do not neglect the most vulnerable.

Where should Africa direct its policy thinking and solutions?

In considering its policy options in pursuing a sustainable development path it is important for Africa to build on its comparative advantages, i.e. abundant labour, a growing middle class, pristine ecological biospheres and abundant natural resources, minerals and vast tracts of arable land. There are at least eight game changers that Africa has to master – or perhaps more realistically, manage – to ensure that it will not remain in perpetuity a continent on the margins of the global economy with growing internal inequality and only brief flowerings of prosperity.

These include combating climate change, accelerating land reform, tackling the digital divide, addressing Africa's enduring infrastructure deficit, pursuing adaptive human resource development and employment creation in the age of greater automation, political and governance reform including managing migration, urbanisation and domestic resource mobilisation. In all eight areas both the private sector and governments have powerful roles to play and the need to creatively engage a variety of new actors in the development space is paramount. As the SDGs illustrate, sustainable development requires a 360 degree approach and indeed all eight game changers listed above are interlinked. I will unpack five of the key game changers below.

Managing the impact of climate change and moving away from a carbon intensive growth path

The move away from fossil fuels will be a major disrupter for many African but also many other oil-producing economies. This is no longer a moot point. For all the speculation about a long tail end to the phasing out of oil and coal as the bedrock of most power generation capacity globally, the adverse impacts of climate change are upon us and Africa is poorly prepared to deal with the negative impacts of inclement weather, searing droughts and disease. However, this is also a unique opportunity for Africa to reframe its energy policy and related infrastructure.

There are at least some positive steps in this direction as seen through the successful roll-out of the independent power producers' programme of the South African government to support a greater uptake of renewable energy in its mainly coal-driven power grid (Department of Energy, 2016). There is the potential to roll-out this initiative across Africa tailoring renewable energy projects for both off-grid and on-grid solutions. The emergence of the Ethiopian government as a major regional champion of hydropower is a second example of what is possible with determined leadership. In both cases, it is clear that given the right policy frameworks, it is possible to unleash the power of the private sector to complement the desire of governments to break the mould. The Ethiopian case also offers useful examples around domestic resource mobilisation, the need to break down complex projects into manageable chunks and the importance of exploring complementary partnerships, such as with China in the infrastructure space.

Addressing the infrastructure gap and the role of domestic resource mobilisation

There is no doubt that economic activity is impossible without sufficient power and an enabling infrastructure, namely roads, rail, airports, harbours, adequate water and sanitation. As noted by the Africa CEO Forum (2014) 'inadequate infrastructure deprives Africa of 2 points of GDP growth annually.' In addition the report noted that private firms would see an improvement in productivity gains of 40% with the appropriate, enabling infrastructure in place.

African countries and infrastructure companies need to approach the massive infrastructure gap in Africa as a major opportunity rather than a constant drag on economic development. The infrastructure sector is able to absorb fairly low-skilled labour in large numbers. It is important that African countries become more equal partners in infrastructure development on the continent. This is entirely possible if there is a greater emphasis on domestic resource mobilisation efforts, skills transfer with the eye on ongoing maintenance and greater local participation in infrastructure projects.

While the emergence of new development finance institutions like the BRICS New Development Bank financing infrastructure is to be welcomed, there should be greater emphasis in African countries on the development of local development finance institutions and infrastructure and other financing instruments (OECD, 2015). The work by institutions like the Collaborative Africa Budget Reform Initiative (CABRI) to improve budget sector reform and tax collection is instrumental in supporting fiscal accountability and transparency (CABRI, 2016). But it is also important that regulatory reforms improve the financial maturity and depth of markets, increases access to banking services and finance (i.e. not only commercial lending) and supports the development of new financial instruments that are appropriate to the African context.

Tackling the digital divide

Technological innovation is able to act as a spring board to leapfrog development, spur economic activity and enhance public participation and accountability. The World Development Report (World Bank 2016a) on technological innovation in the digital age is illustrative of the potential of technological innovation and digital access to spur economic development. This is an area that African governments need to prioritise given its power to shrink in real time geographical distances between societies, firms and people. Digital access could be a game changer for African societies if managed well, enabling the development of local entrepreneurs and start-ups, the improvement of firm performance and consumer choice and the roll-out of education and training and e-health services at a fraction of the traditional costs linked to these services. Digital access also enables faster adaptive learning, which will be essential in the new job market where life-long learning will be a critical determinant of job security.

Accelerating land reform

Another important area that African countries ignore at their peril is the nascent ability of Africa to become the breadbasket of the world. Agriculture and agribusiness have been put forward by various studies as one of the most important ways that African countries can move up the value chain. Highly labour intensive, with some automation possibilities upstream, this sector has the potential to position many African economies on a more sustainable growth path. It is important that land tenure is adequately addressed along with proper agriculture support programmes appropriate to emerging farmers. In addition, countries should focus on preserving their bio-diversity. There is a trade-off to manage in covering vast parts of Africa with the latest strains of drought resistance crops versus responsible guardianship of some of the most diverse biospheres on the planet. Sustainable use of wildlife is a term that is particularly emphasised by Africa's policy makers, but it is important not to neglect the income generating potential of the tourism sector, another major labour absorptive sector for Africa. Lastly, while a relatively slow growing China of 6% of GDP is not in any way comparable with the 14% average experienced over the last decade, this represents healthy demand for African resources and a sound base on which to exploit Africa's mineral resources with greater regard for the environment.

Thus the capacity to exploit labour absorbing sectors in Africa, that are not necessarily only linked to extractives, raises the question of whether premature de-industrialisation need be such a major factor. Instead, there seems to be a strong argument emerging that a growing middle class in Africa would stimulate the development of the domestic services sector. This is an important opportunity for both African and developed economies and raises questions around the rather pessimistic view that migration is primarily driven by conflict.

Migration as a positive driver of development

We accept that South-North migration is a fait accompli for a variety of reasons, no less because of the incidence of conflict. However, as the recent global financial crisis also showed, skilled labour is incredibly mobile. We have seen this with Portuguese and Spanish migration to Africa and South America following the impact of the 2008 financial crisis. While some European countries are discussing the introduction of a basic income grant and the reduction of working hours, others are increasing the retirement age. Yet on the other side of the world there is a huge demand for education and health services, in addition to other professional services such as engineering, actuary, legal, financial etc. The broader question therefore is whether over the next 15 years and in fact until 2050 the current trend will not strengthen further, i.e. a proliferation of South-South, North-South and South-North migration. With rising income levels in Africa, but also because of its significant skills deficit, it is incumbent on African governments to introduce smart labour legislation that enables the sourcing and retention of skilled labour.

The big question is what will the societal implications be? Are we ready for closer forms of integration, a smaller world, but at the same time less formalised to counter the fragmentary forces emerging in the European project? It remains an open question what the trend in Africa will be compared to other regions in supporting functional co-operation. It is in this respect that governance norms become crucial, both economically and politically, as well as support of regional norms and partnerships to support collaboration across great divides.

A sober assessment of the development path that Africa will need to charter over the next 15 years underscores the importance of determined leadership, political will, pragmatism, resilience and resourcefulness.

Section 4. Azerbaijan: an economy trapped in the Caucasus. The next 15 years between the Russian Federation, Turkey and Iran
Vugar Bayramov[4] and Ahmad Alili[5]

Azerbaijan has a similar background to other Commonwealth of Independent States (CIS) countries in the South Caucasus and Central Asia, such as the Russian Federation, Kazakhstan and Turkmenistan. During the period of 2000-15, it experienced a similar path of economic growth, fostered by high oil and gas prices; and stagnation over the past two years, under declining oil prices.

The oil income has strikingly affected Azerbaijan's path of economic development for the past 15 years. Now, following the slump in oil prices, the country is experiencing a completely different set of conditions. This is the perfect time to forecast the economic trends for Azerbaijan for the next 15 years. Since Azerbaijan is trapped in a sensitive geopolitical region – the Caucasus – the importance of forecasting and the ability to adapt to the quickly changing international environment is vital.

This article analyses the economic and policy agenda of Azerbaijan for the next 15 years. First, it presents a brief preview of the current economic trends, and explains the challenges. In the following section, the article presents recommendations.

Before proceeding with the forecasting, two points should be made clear. First, the growth model, which worked for the country for the previous 15-year period, is no longer effective. Forecasting based on previous trends is impossible, simply because the trends have been reversed. During 2000-15, Azerbaijan experienced rapid economic development. It was mainly attributed to the exploitation of oil and gas basins in the Caspian Sea. During this period, oil revenues constituted nearly half of the country's GDP. Thanks to the oil revenues, in 2006-07, the country experienced the highest increase in economic growth in its history – averaging 29.8% (Asian Development Bank, 2014).

In terms of economic growth, 2015 was not a favourable year for Azerbaijan. Slumping oil prices significantly affected the macroeconomic indicators of the country. The first sign was the devaluation of the national currency – the manat – followed by the decrease in the Central Bank reserves by USD 8.74 billion, equivalent to the five-year accumulation. Considerable declines in GDP and income of the population, negative shifts in the labour market, and the substantial effect of the devaluation of the national currency on the banking sector indicate serious problems in the national economy (Center for Economic and Social Development, 2016). 2015 was a trend-changing year, pushing the government to instigate reforms.

Second, the economic agenda in Azerbaijan heavily depends on the geopolitical agenda of the country. Studies on the political determinants of economic reforms in former Soviet Union countries indicate a "strong correlation between the progress in political and economic reforms" (Dabrowski and Radzislawa, 2002). Also, studies indicate the greater role of the Russian Federation in forming the political and reform agenda in "non-Baltic Post-Soviet states", while the EU played a prominent role in prompting some of the Eastern European Countries to undergo liberal economic reforms (Cameron and Orenstein, 2013).

Located in the Caucasus, between the Russian Federation, Turkey and the Islamic Republic of Iran (hereafter, Iran), the political and hence reform agenda in Azerbaijan is heavily influenced by these actors. Left with little oil revenues in the upcoming years, the surrounding nations, and the political-economic agenda in these countries, will strongly influence economic trends in Azerbaijan over the next 15 years.

The prognosis on the Russian Federation's future for the following 15 years is usually accompanied with pessimistic notes (Stratfor, 2015). Unlike the Russian Federation, Iran – having reached a deal over its nuclear programme – is expected to attract more foreign investment and economic growth. Immigrants from Azerbaijan would usually choose Russia as the main immigration destination. Following the change of economic fortunes, Iran might become a new destination for Azerbaijani job migration, and hence source of remittances. It might ultimately affect the political landscape of the country also (Alili, 2015). The World Bank's Doing Business indicators also show challenges for the economy in Azerbaijan. Getting credit, dealing with construction permits, getting electricity and trading across borders are among the areas to be improved for attracting investment (World Bank, 2016b).

Nevertheless, the next 15 years will provide new opportunities for Azerbaijan. The World Economic Forum's recent Global Competitiveness Report (WEF, 2016) gives Azerbaijan the best ranking among CIS countries. This should create additional opportunities over the coming 15 years.

So, for the post-oil period, policy makers should anticipate dramatic changes. Due to declining oil prices, politically important actors in the region may increase their leverage over the political and economic life of the country. It creates a completely new set of challenges for the country, which should be tackled.

Azerbaijan needs economic reforms. Future prospects depend on how nimbly the government will liberalise the economy, and thereby allowing foreign direct investment to flow in.

To resolve these problems, the following recommendations are suggested:

1. Diversifying the set of economic partners and lessening dependency on Turkey, Iran and the Russian Federation, by liberalising the economy. Strengthening economic ties with the EU can play a crucial role in diversifying Azerbaijan's set of partners. Signing a new Co-operation Agreement with the EU should be the top policy agenda for the government.

2. Improving good governance and human rights. It is crucial to enhance citizens' well-being, the functioning of institutions and in turn spur greater interest for investment into Azerbaijan and greater linkages with the OECD countries.

3. Accelerating WTO accession. This will lead to increased predictability of economic development in Azerbaijan, enhanced transparency and reduced corruption. WTO accession will create new opportunities for the business sector and also open foreign markets to the local goods. It will lead to more competition in domestic markets and access to innovative technology.

4. Committing to structural reforms and improving the business environment is necessary to increase competitiveness in the country. Advancing reforms in customs and the public finance system is very important for attracting foreign investment.

5. Liberalising the public financial sector and creating measures to counter the volatility of the national currency will play an important role for local business development.

Notes

1. Alan Hirsch is Professor of Development Policy and Practice and has directed the Graduate School of Development Policy and Practice at University of Cape Town since 2013.
2. Donald Mmari (Ph.D) is the Executive Director of REPOA in Tanzania.
3. Neuma Grobbelaar is the Research Director of the South African Institute of International Affairs (SAIIA), a leading African Foreign policy think tank based at the University of the Witwatersrand.
4. Vugar Bayramov (Ph.D) is the Chairman of Centre for Economic and Social Development (CESD) in Azerbaijan.
5. Ahmad Alili is a Senior Researcher at the Centre for Economic and Social Development (CESD).

References

Africa CEO Forum (2014), "The private sector, driving force of Africa's growth", organised by Groupe Jeune Afrique in partnership with the African Development Bank (ABD) and Rainbow Unlimited, Geneva, 19 March 2014, https://www2.deloitte.com/content/dam/Deloitte/fpc/Documents/nous-connaitre/deloitte-afrique-francophone/deloitte_africa-ceo-forum-the-private-sector-driving-force.pdf.

Alili, A. (2015), "Azerbaijan and Iran after the Sanctions: The Pathways of Advanced Engagement and Confrontation", *Russkii Vopros*, http://cesd.az/new/wp-content/uploads/2016/01/Azerbaijan-and-Iran-after-the-Sanctions.pdf.

Arora, V. and V. Athanasios (2005), "The Implications of South African Economic Growth for the Rest of Africa", *IMF Working Paper*, African and European Departments https://www.imf.org/external/pubs/ft/wp/2005/wp0558.pdf.

Asian Development Bank (2014), *Azerbaijan: Country Partnership Strategy (2014-2018)*, https://www.adb.org/sites/default/files/institutional-document/81989/cps-aze-2014-2018-0.pdf.

Bhorat, H. (2016), "Inequality in Africa: Implications for Sustainable Development Goals", *Brookings Brief*.

Cameron, D.R., and Orenstein, M.A. (May 2013), "Post-Soviet Authoritarianism: The Influence of Russia in Its "Near Abroad", *Post-Soviet Affairs*, Vol. 28, No. 1, pp.1-44, DOI: 10.2747/1060-586X.28.1.1

Center for Economic and Social Development. (2016), *The Economy of Azerbaijan in 2015: Independent View*, CESD Press, Baku, Azerbaijan, http://cesd.az/new/wp-content/uploads/2016/01/CESD_Research_Paper_Azerbaijan_Economy_2015.pdf.

Collaborative Africa Budget Reform Initiative (2016), http://www.cabri-sbo.org/, accessed 17 September 2016.

Dabrowski, M. and G. Radzislawa (2002), "Political Determinants of Economic Reforms in Former Communist Countries", *CASE Network Studies and Analyses*, No. 242. http://ssrn.com/abstract=1440725.

Department of Energy, Republic of South Africa (2016), *Renewable Energy Independent Power Producer Procurement Programme*, http://www.ipprenewables.co.za/.

Hausmann, R., L. Pritchard and D. Rodrik (2005), "Growth Accelerations", *Journal of Economic Growth*, Vol. 10, pp. 303-29, DOI: 10.1007/s10887-005-4712-0.

IMF (2016), *Regional Policy Outlook Sub-Saharan Africa April 2016: Time for a Policy Reset* https://www.imf.org/external/pubs/ft/reo/2016/afr/eng/sreo0416.htm.

Nalishebo, S. and A. Halwampa (2015), "A Cautionary Tale of Zambia's International Sovereign Bond Issuances", *Zambia Institute of Policy Analysis and Research (ZIPAR) Working Paper No.22*, March, http://www.zipar.org.zm/index.php?option=com_docman&view=download&alias=44-a-cautionary-tale-of-zambia-s-international-sovereign-bond-issuances&category_slug=working-papers&Itemid=120.

Narreinen, S.P. (2013), "Industrialisation: The Mauritian Model" in J.E Stiglitz, J. Yu Lin and E. Patel (eds.), *The Industrial Policy Revolution II: Africa in the 21st Century*, Palgrave Macmillan, London.

OECD (2015), *Infrastructure Financing Instruments and Incentives*, OECD Publishing, Paris. http://www.oecd.org/daf/fin/private-pensions/Infrastructure-Financing-Instruments-and-Incentives.pdf.

Oqubay, A. (2015), *Made in Africa: Industrial Policy in Ethiopia*, Oxford University Press, Oxford.

Page, J. (2016), "Sustaining Domestic Growth: Structural transformation depends on Jobs, Industry and SMEs", *Foresight Africa: Top Priorities for the Continent in 2016*, Brookings Institution, https://www.brookings.edu/wp-content/uploads/2016/01/foresightafrica2016_fullreport.pdf.

Roe, A.R. and S. Dodd (2016), "Like it or not, poor countries are increasingly dependent on mining and oil & gas, *United Nations University*, June 2016, https://www.wider.unu.edu/publication/it-or-not-poor-countries-are-increasingly-dependent-mining-and-oil-gas.

Stratfor (2015), *Decade Forecast: 2015-2025*, https://www.stratfor.com/forecast/decade-forecast-2015-2025.

Sy, A. (2016), "Managing Economic Shocks: African Prospects in the Evolving Global Environment", *Foresight Africa: Top Priorities for the Continent in 2016*, Brookings Institution, https://www.brookings.edu/wp-content/uploads/2016/01/foresightafrica2016_fullreport.pdf.

Tanzania National Bureau of Statistics (2014), *The 2014 Integrated Labour Force Survey (ILFS) – Analytical Report*, TNBS, Dar es Salaam, http://www.nbs.go.tz/nbstz/index.php/english/statistics-by-subject/labour-statistics/614-the-2014-integrated-labour-force-survey-ilfs.

United Nations Economic Commission for Africa (2010), *Economic Report on Africa 2010. Promoting high-level sustainable growth to reduce unemployment in Africa*, UN Economic Commission for Africa, Addis Ababa, http://www.un.org/en/africa/osaa/pdf/pubs/2010era-uneca.pdf.

World Bank (2016a), *Digital Dividends*, World Development Report, World Bank Group, Washington, DC., http://documents.worldbank.org/curated/en/896971468194972881/pdf/102725-PUB-Replacement-PUBLIC.pdf.

World Bank (2016b), *Doing Business 2016. Measuring Regulatory Quality and Efficiency*, World Bank, Washington, DC, DOI: 10.1596/978-1-4648-0667-4.

World Economic Forum (2016), *Global Competitiveness Report (2016-17)*, http://www3.weforum.org/docs/GCR2016-2017/05FullReport/TheGlobalCompetitivenessReport2016-2017_FINAL.pdf.

World Economic Forum (2015), *The Global Competitiveness Report 2015-2016*, World Economic Forum, Geneva, http://www3.weforum.org/docs/gcr/2015-2016/Global_Competitiveness_Report_2015-2016.pdf.

Chapter 3

Risks and opportunities for inclusive societies in developing and emerging countries

Chapter 3 is concerned with inclusive societies in developing and emerging economies. Rapid demographic transitions, urbanisation, jobless growth and premature deindustrialisation are placing huge pressure on the development of cohesive societies. Citizens of developing countries, and particularly young people, are growing increasingly disaffected as inequality rises, and un- and underemployment grow. René N'Guettia Kouassi's piece focuses on the problem of growing inequality across the world. Gilbert Houngbo discusses the rise of young people in informal employment globally and potential policy solutions to this problem. Samir Saran and Vivan Sharan also tackle informality but from the perspective of India; they argue that technology could play a role in ameliorating it. Finally, Hussein Al-Majali analyses the lack of opportunities for youth in the MENA region and how political leaders there need to build a new conception of "active citizenship".

Chapter 2 was largely preoccupied with how the structural transformation of emerging economies can be catalysed, and the risks and challenges associated with this undertaking in the new macroeconomic environment. Chapter 3 focuses on inclusive societies – specifically, issues of inequality, creating enough secure jobs to match the population growth that many developing regions are experiencing and providing adequate measures of social protection for their populations.

The overview chapter identified demographic transitions – specifically the rapid growth of working-age populations in sub-Saharan Africa and South Asia – as a major global risk over the coming 15 years if not managed appropriately. Creating jobs will be difficult as GDP growth and employment is decoupling across countries of all income categories. People in developing regions are on the move in the search for jobs, both within countries to cities as urbanisation continues rapidly and internationally, increasingly to higher-income OECD countries. Fragile states also are giving rise to terrorist organisations such as Boko Harem in Nigeria and Al-Shabaab in Somalia. The quest for social inclusion will be a key development challenge in such highly fraught economic and political climates.

The authors of the articles in this chapter are concerned with different aspects of this quest for social inclusion. One cross-cutting theme is creating opportunities for youth in the context of youth informality and under/unemployment. The authors use varying approaches to explore this theme. Gilbert Houngbo highlights the plight of the working youth globally: young people are over-represented in the informal economy and informal employment imposes legacy costs on youth throughout their working lives. Hussein Al-Majali looks at the relative lack of youth opportunities in the MENA region, which is experiencing severe political turbulence. Here, a lack of jobs and the absence of a meaningful political response to young people's demands and expectations are fuelling dissatisfaction and alienation. The solutions to these problems are complex and require patience. Houngbo recommends education and training programmes that facilitate the school-to-work transition and correct skills mismatches, and the implementation of labour policies based on international standards to ensure young people receive equal treatment and are afforded rights at work. Al-Majali emphasises the need for labour market reforms and government delivery of high-quality Science, Technology, Engineering and Mathematics (STEM) education and vocational training to provide disaffected youth with meaningful opportunities.

Samir Saran and Vivan Sharan argue that technology can be used to facilitate inclusiveness in India by extending social protection mechanisms to informal workers. By digitally identifying workers, the government can provide workers with income security, the availability of health, retirement and life insurance coverage, and safe and healthy working conditions, thus ushering in a "new formality".

Finally, René N'Guettia Kouassi contends that growing inequality within and between countries is a major global risk and will worsen if left unchecked. Kouassi recommends improving social protection programmes to reduce inequality and increase aid inclusiveness.

The sections in this chapter highlight the risks and challenges that divided and unequal societies pose, and recommend a variety of policy solutions to help make them more inclusive. The contributions to this chapter neither represent the positions of the Development Centre nor the OECD, but are solely the authors' own views.

Section 1. The unequal distribution of wealth in the world: the major issue of the 21st century
René N'Guettia Kouassi[1]

Today it is little secret that the world is marked by growing within country inequality (UNDP, 2013). This inequality extends to the distribution of resources between countries, within countries and amongst countries' regions. Natural resources, production capacities and infrastructure are often unevenly distributed within continents, regions, countries and even amongst regions within a country. The substantial gap in living conditions prevailing in the world could thus, in part, be attributed to differences in resource endowments and wealth creation capabilities. Climatic conditions, access to social services, hunger and malnutrition are all factors that tangibly demonstrate the geographic dimensions of development. The wealth produced must be distributed equitably as remuneration of labour used in the production process.

Despite significant growth in developing countries over recent years, and persistent economic stagnation in developed countries, the gap between rich and poor is so entrenched that the issue of wealth distribution merits renewed attention. To illustrate, it is estimated that 1% of the world population owns 40% of the wealth and the poorest 50% hold only 1% of global wealth (UNRISD, 2012). To curb the existing economic disparities within countries, between countries and between regions of the world new wealth distribution mechanisms need to be implemented. In other words, contemporary global institutions such as the United Nations must innovate wealth distribution mechanisms to achieve a more peaceful and prosperous world. With this in mind, the United Nations must develop wealth distribution mechanisms that ensure peace among people regardless of their colour, religion and place of residence. One of the reasons for such a response is that the problem of inequality is also a question of political stability and social cohesion. Viewed within the context of the migration crisis and the escalation of global conflicts, a more economically equal distribution would reduce the massive flow of economic migrants and allay some of the social tensions that derive from inequality in the first place.

Good economic and political governance, innovative redistribution policies, and the creation of decent jobs should receive more attention in all countries.

Moreover, improving social protection programs can reduce inequality. States and institutions must fight against economic disparity in tandem with their development objectives since inequality itself can be an impediment to growth. However, the measures taken towards more equitable wealth distribution must not disincentivise the rich from taking up their productive activities, nor create any other perverse effects on local or global growth.

Improved co-operation between developed and developing countries would be beneficial for all. International institutions must abandon the post-WWII logic of paternalistic humanitarianism. For a more peaceful world, development issues must be studied through the lens of the egalitarian distribution of wealth.

Section 2. Young and informal employment
Gilbert Houngbo[2]

Young people around the world continue to suffer disproportionately from the lack of decent work and low-quality jobs measured in terms of working poverty, low pay and/or employment status, and exposure to occupational hazards and injury. Globally, half of the labour force is working and producing in the informal economy (ILO, 2015a), with an over-representation of young men and women. Recent studies indicate that labour informality is more common in some types of employment status, jobs, sectors and sizes of enterprises. Likewise, these characteristics, together with those typical of the profile of new workers – who lack work experience and high productivity early on in their careers – make youth a particularly vulnerable group (ILO, 2014a). While there are some common trends among countries with respect to the persistence of informality and its particularly high incidence among youth, each country also has characteristics specific to its labour markets.

The informal economy thrives in a context of weak formal job creation and precarious work, poverty and gender inequality. For hundreds of millions of young men and women, the immediate disadvantages of informality go beyond lower wages, less job stability and a lack of social coverage. The effects of informal employment may potentially extend throughout individuals' working lives. Strong evidence shows that when youth enter the informal labour market, they are penalised throughout their working lives.

The magnitude of informality in youth employment

Based on School-to-Work Transition Survey (SWTS) data from 20 countries, three-fourths (75.4%) of young workers aged 15-29 are engaged in informal employment at the aggregate level (Table 3.1). There are, however, important variations across countries and regions. Young workers have the greatest chance to work formally in Eastern Europe and, to a certain degree, the Middle East (Jordan only) and Latin America and the Caribbean (with exceptions of El Salvador and Peru). In the sub- Saharan African countries, in contrast, from eight to nine in ten young workers are in informal employment. Shares of informality seem to be closely linked to the economic wealth of the country; the aggregate youth informal employment share among low- income countries is well above that of upper-middle income countries (90.8 and 62.0%, respectively) (Shehu and Nilsson, 2014).

The composition of informal employment also shows a dramatic shift as national income levels increase. Informal employment among youth in low-income countries is strongly focused around employment in the informal sector, while shares in informal jobs in the formal sector are low. In the upper-middle income countries except Jamaica and the Russian Federation, in contrast, higher shares of informally employed youth are engaged in the formal sector than the informal sector (Ibid.).

Table 3.1. Share of informal and formal employment in youth employment and breakdown of youth informal employment, 20 countries (%)

		Share in youth employment		Share in informal employment	
		Informal employment	Formal employment	Employed in informal sector	Informal job in formal sector
Asia & the Pacific	Cambodia	98.3	1.7	68.8	31.2
	Samoa	67.7	32.3	100.0	0.0
	Viet Nam	76.4	23.6	54.6	45.4
Eastern Europe	Armenia	64.2	35.8	37.1	62.9
	Former Yugoslav Republic of Macedonia	48.4	51.6	43.7	56.3
	Russia - 11 regions	50.9	49.1	52.8	47.2
	Ukraine	57.1	42.9	19.8	80.2

Table 3.1. Share of informal and formal employment in youth employment and breakdown of youth informal employment, 20 countries (%) *(cont.)*

		Share in youth employment		Share in informal employment	
		Informal employment	Formal employment	Employed in informal sector	Informal job in formal sector
Latin America & the Caribbean	Brazil	61.6	38.4	47.6	52.4
	El Salvador	91.8	8.2	64.0	36.0
	Jamaica	75.3	24.7	55.8	44.2
	Peru	83.5	16.5	37.3	62.7
Middle East & North Africa	Egypt	91.1	8.9	36.5	63.5
	Jordan	46.8	53.2	21.6	78.4
Sub-Saharan Africa	Benin	89.7	10.3	89.9	10.1
	Liberia	82.5	17.5	77.0	23.0
	Malawi	96.3	3.7	93.9	6.1
	Tanzania	87.5	12.5	66.2	33.8
	Togo	89.1	10.9	85.9	14.1
	Uganda	92.1	7.9	86.3	13.7
	Zambia	94.7	5.3	83.1	16.9
Aggregate, 20 countries		75.4	24.6	55.1	44.9
Aggregate, 7 low-income countries		90.8	9.2	81.2	18.8
Aggregate, 7 low-income countries		81.0	19.0	62.5	37.5
Aggregate, 7 upper-middle income countries		62.0	38.0	43.7	56.3

Note: Income groupings are based on the World Bank classification.
Source: Authors' calculations using SWTS data from 20 countries. Shehu, Erin, Nilsson, Björn (2014), Informal employment among youth: evidence from 20 school-to-work transition surveys.

The challenges of formalising young employment and implications on youth

Across all regions, the major challenge is that informality and youth are closely linked. Both the informal and formal sectors contribute to the high rates of informality among youth. Informality is posing serious challenges to the quality of employment and the socio-economic outcomes among youth.

Evidence shows that the average wage of the informally employed youth is lower than that of the formally employed youth. Regarding the components of informal employment, the average hourly wage for jobs in the informal sector is lower than the average wage for informal jobs in the formal sector. The self-employed operating in the informal sector, on average, earn less than those operating formally. In the 20 countries analysed using SWTS data, employers have higher earnings than own- account workers. However, there are exceptions to this rule, especially for sub-Saharan African countries (Shehu and Nilsson, 2014).

In terms of job quality, Table 3.2 shows the rate of time-related underemployment for the formally and informally employed youth. At the aggregate level, underemployment is higher among the informally employed. The underemployed represent 12.5% of the informally employed youth and only 6.2% of the formally employed youth. Looking at the components of informal employment, underemployment is more widespread among those who work in the informal sector and less common among those working informally in the formal sector. A regional perspective indicates that time-related underemployment is more pronounced among the informally employed in Latin America and sub-Saharan Africa, and less pronounced in Eastern Europe and the MENA region (Ibid.).

Table 3.2. Rate of time-related underemployment among informally and formally employed youth

Country	Employed in informal sector	Informal job in formal sector	Informal employment	Formal employment
			%	
Armenia	17.3	8.2	11.6	9.7
Benin	9.6	15.5	10.2	2.5
Brazil	24.4	8.8	16.2	7
Cambodia	11.4	9.2	10.7	4.4
Egypt	5.5	6.2	5.9	3.1
El Salvador	23.7	19.1	22.1	3.3
Former Yugoslav Republic of Macedonia	21.3	5.8	12.6	3.1
Jamaica	21.8	17.4	19.9	4.8
Jordan	4.7	1.6	2.3	2.3
Liberia	15.7	9.9	14.4	9.8
Malawi	14.4	15.6	14.5	14.9
Peru	25.6	12.3	17.3	8.1
Samoa	0.5		0.5	0
Tanzania	18.8	9.4	15.6	16.8
Togo	22.2	15.6	21.2	9.4
Uganda	16.0	9.7	15.2	14.6
Ukraine	11.1	4.5	5.8	4.6
Viet Nam	12.0	3.7	8.2	1.6
Zambia	21.2	13.3	19.8	18.6
Aggregate (19 countries)	16.6	7.6	12.5	6.2

Source: Authors' calculations using SWTS data from 19 countries. Shehu, Erin, Nilsson, Björn (2014), Informal employment among youth: evidence from 20 school-to-work transition surveys.

Concerning job satisfaction, the informally employed are less satisfied with their jobs in all countries except Liberia. In general, job satisfaction is low in sub-Saharan Africa and relatively high in Latin America. An alternative measure of job satisfaction was proposed; data showed that the informally employed more often desire to change jobs, the main reason evoked being to earn a higher income.

The characteristics associated with informal employment - having lower average wages, having lower job satisfaction and being more likely to being underemployed – continue throughout an individual's working life. Young people represent the promise of changing societies for the better. Yet, there are not enough jobs for young people and informal employment amongst young people remains pervasive (ILO, 2012).

The ILO school-work surveys carried out in Brazil, El Salvador, Jamaica and Peru found that only a small percentage of youth transition from school to formal employment. Youths' educational level is important both in terms of immediate results as well as in the short and long term. The lack of completion of basic schooling hastens youths' incorporation in the labour market, impeding them from attaining a higher educational level, which is a highly-valued attribute when they initially enter the labour market (ILO, 2013). The advantages youth have before the transition, including a higher level of education and income, are replicated in the transition to the formal labour market since this group had a greater chance of obtaining formal employment in all the countries analysed.

To conclude this section, entering the labour force informally has repercussions for young workers that go beyond the labour relationship. Lower wages, employment instability, precarious working conditions, and a lack of social security coverage, social representation and dialogue make young workers vulnerable and severely limit their personal development and that of their families. In response, an increasing number of developing countries have developed several policies that range from national plans to targeted interventions using legal instruments, public programmes and agreements with social actors, among others.

Policy options for youth transitioning from the informal to the formal economy

The fact that youth informality is gaining ground (ILO, 2015b) and remains a crucial development challenge does not mean the absence of innovative policy frameworks to facilitate the transition from the informal to the formal economy and boost productive employment. Emerging and developing countries are searching for new policies and practical responses in order to promote decent work for millions of young men and women who are engaged in the informal economy.

In response to the challenges of youth employment and informality, the ILO constituents adopted two important policy instruments at the International Labour Conference (ILC) in 2012 and 2015 respectively. These two policy instruments align with each other and reinforce the clear policy guidance on youth employment and their transition from the informal to the formal economy.

In 2012, the ILO adopted a Resolution calling for immediate, targeted and renewed action to tackle the youth employment crisis with taking considerations of the following policy areas:

- Pro-employment macroeconomic policies that support stronger aggregate demand and improve access to finance
- Education and training that facilitate the school-to-work transition and that correct skills mismatches
- Labour market policies that favour employment of disadvantaged youth
- Entrepreneurship and self-employment for aspiring young entrepreneurs
- Labour policies based on international standards to ensure young people receive equal treatment and are afforded rights at work (ILO, 2015c)

More importantly, the ILC adopted the Recommendation no, 204 concerning the transition from the informal to the formal economy in 2015. This is the first international labour standard to focus on the informal economy in its entirety and diversity and to point clearly to the transition to the formal economy as the means for realising decent work for all and achieving inclusive development. The Recommendation, of universal relevance, acknowledges the broad diversity of situations of informality, including specific national contexts and priorities for the transition to the formal economy, and provides practical guidance to address these priorities. It stresses the need to pay special attention to those who are especially vulnerable to the most serious decent work deficits in the informal economy, including young people.

In emerging and developing economies, the challenge of the transition to the formal economy is closely linked to the challenge of development and productive transformation of the economy. From this perspective, it is important to note that Recommendation No. 204 acknowledges that most people enter the informal economy not by choice but as a consequence of a lack of opportunities in the formal economy and in the absence of other means of livelihood. Therefore, in a context of poverty and multifaceted vulnerabilities, policy efforts to facilitate the transition to formality should go hand in hand with ensuring opportunities for income security, livelihoods and entrepreneurship.

Consensus regarding best practices to address informality is that integrated strategies should be adopted. Interventions are more effective when they are combined, given that this practice allows them to address diversity as well as the scale of the informal economy and informal employment in the formal sector (ILO, 2014b). Evidence indicates that the greatest reduction in informality rates occurs when the set of instruments used is broader and more comprehensive (ILO, 2014a).

The selected formalisation policies included in such integrated strategies fall mainly into three categories. The first includes measures or *incentives for the creation of formal jobs and conditions for their development*, such as subsidies for the development or expansion of enterprises and of employment, and programmes designed to increase skills of the labour force. The second category covers initiatives *specifically designed to formalise informal jobs and units*, such as registration programmes, labour inspection plans and support to the formalisation of low-productivity microenterprises. Finally, the third category brings together initiatives to *extend social coverage to informal workers*, even without the formalisation of their jobs, including social protection programmes that offer unemployment benefits, health care coverage and maternity protection.

Activities to create quality jobs are frequently implemented as part of the initiatives to eliminate youth informality. These measures are distinguished between those that act as incentives on labour demand and those that focus on supply. The former attempt to compensate for the disadvantages youth face in terms of work experience and limited productivity when they search for employment. To this end, they provide economic benefits to employers to encourage them to provide formal contracts to workers or to support employers through technical assistance and financing for enterprise development –particularly in less developed areas of a country. Incentives targeting supply concentrate on giving youth the assets they need to overcome barriers to accessing formal employment, such as technical and soft skills and the accreditation of work experience. The most common incentives for labour demand are wage subsidies for hiring youth, which generally target low-income individuals. In some countries, these subsidies are specifically assigned when youth are hired. Others call for general subsidies for hiring personnel for a specific size of enterprise or sector and in cases where youth actively participate.

Experiences developed in Argentina, Brazil, Chile, Colombia, Mexico and Uruguay are examples of policies providing subsidies for hiring youth or that have a potential impact on this group. Some of these initiatives link the hiring subsidy with training activities to be provided by the employer or under the responsibility of the young workers, establishing it as a condition. The objective is to guarantee that on-the-job training complements formal education during the formative years, when the process of human capital accumulation is more intense.

Conclusion

In developing countries, informality and youth are closely linked and youth informal employment is widespread. Both the informal and formal sectors contribute to the high rates of informal employment among youth. Informally employed youth have lower wages, less job security and fewer labour rights. While informally employed youth with a better socioeconomic and educational background have the best chances of transitioning to formal employment, informally employed youth without these advantages are especially vulnerable to remaining informal.

The characteristics of informality and of youth offer an opportunity to implement a wide range of policies. Current initiatives focus on overcoming the barriers that come between youth and decent work, adopting different approaches to increasing formal employment and discouraging informal employment. While policy responses for young informal workers are for many the same as those established for other workers, they have also led to initiatives to promote formal job creation specifically for youth. Even though impact evaluation on public policies aiming at youth transition to formality is limited across regions, the few impact evaluations conducted in Latin America and the Caribbean region show positive effects in terms of formalising employment among youth (ILO, 2015d).

Promoting formal employment among youth requires, in the one hand, aligning programmes, legislation and national plans with this aim and, in the other hand, broad-based and comprehensive policies which are reducing informality levels more effectively than sole specific initiatives to promote formal employment (ILO, 2014b). Finally, the ongoing challenge in policy analysis is to consider information as a critical resource. The experiences of countries cannot be enriched and their performance cannot improve as long as knowledge gaps remain with regard to what works and for whom.

Section 3. The future of the Indian workforce
Samir Saran[3] and Vivan Sharan[4]

The informal economy is growing in India, and that may be a good thing. Even as policy makers around the world attempt to grapple with challenges linked to labour productivity and ageing, India's circumstances are unique. By 2030, when most major countries will have middle aged or elderly workforces, India's will still be young. Around 36% of the Indian population in 2011-12 was 17 years or younger and around 13% was between 18 and 24 years (Table 3.3). The informal economy also accounted for nearly half of the employment for those between 18 and 24. Therefore, the discussion on the future of India's informal workforce must be brought to the forefront when discussing growth, employment, sustainability and poverty eradication efforts.

Table 3.3. **Age groups and break downs of population and workforce, 2011-12**

Age group (in years)	% of total population in corresponding age group	Workforce as % of population in each group	Informal workforce as % of workforce
0-17	35.91	3.01	50.5
18-24	12.7	41.49	48.1
25-59	43.22	63.09	46.6
>= 60	8.17	34.48	36.8

Source: 68th Round, National Sample Survey @ Observer Research Foundation's India Data Labs.

The informal economy has long been a subject of policy apathy in India. It has remained outside the remit of most welfare initiatives, and therefore millions have been deprived of even the most basic social security cover and human dignity. In addition, discriminatory and illegal practices followed in the informal sector – like child labour, long working hours and unsafe work conditions, gender violence and abuse – have been difficult to address. India's policy approach towards the informal sector has been to pretend that it does not exist or at best that it can be 'legislated' away. Consequently, the policy discourse has seen informality as a 'bad thing'.

But the public and private sectors in India cannot wish away this constituency and its specific needs, just as the government cannot make it disappear with another act of parliament. India is unlikely to miraculously develop the capacity to absorb 12 million new workers who enter the job market each year. To put it in context, only a cumulative total of around three million jobs have been created by the information technology industry, which has been the torchbearer of the Indian economy since its liberalisation in the early nineties. And relatively fewer public sector jobs are available today. The informal economy on the other hand has been the largest destination for those seeking work and aspiring for more.

What does this mean for policy makers?

In a research project undertaken for the International Labour Organisation (ILO), the authors contend that for India to harness its 'demographic dividend', a 'new formality' of workers and jobs has to be conceived of. Since nearly half of the employment in India's service sector continues to be informal (Table 3.4), and the sector remains the primary driver of productivity growth, it is argued that services sector will be the arena where we can discover 'new formality' and leverage its potentiality.

Table 3.4. Size of informal economy and sector wise distribution by age group, 2011-12, (%)

Age Group (in Years)	Agriculture	Manufacture/Mining	Services
0-17	11.1	60.2	27
18-24	7.9	51.7	39.4
25-59	10	41.1	48.1
>= 60	17.5	34.7	46.7

Source: 68th Round, National Sample Survey @ Observer Research Foundation's India Data Labs.

A formal workforce is typically characterised by jobs that are regulated and protected by the state. Therefore, presence of a formal workforce or jobs is contingent on capacity related aspects including those related to the state's ability to provide social security and regulate diversified sets of economic activities that may be carried out by large or small businesses; and the ability of enterprises to generate employment in consonance with regulatory stipulations.

Based on the above, 'a' contextual definition of what we allude to as the 'new formal' in India's case (and of some other similarly situated economies), would essentially provide each worker a reasonable degree of income level and security (*minimum wages*), availability of health, retirement and life insurance cover (*critical needs*) and safe and congenial working conditions (*safety*). In essence, if the informal worker can be assured (and insured) of these three qualifying criteria, we would have achieved this "new formality". However, this is counterintuitive, and goes against the grain of both development economics and the literature dealing with labour and employment. The dominant discourse still espouses the virtues of transition to formal workspaces and the formal economy as a significant determinant of economic progress.

However, this discourse does not account for the disruptive role of technology and/or the potential of the digital economy and of digitisation and digitally driven supply chains that span the breadth of nations and transcend national boundaries. In particular, it does not take into account the nature of the expanding digital economy workspace where there is likely to be greater mobilisation of the informal workforce alongside the positive effect on gender gap in employment – two trends that also played out in advanced countries in the early parts of the last century, when the industrial economy expanded there.

It also fails to recognise that the deployment of technology to complement national development agendas allows us to bring in a degree of formal guarantees to the informal employment terms. Technology allows us the ability to identify each worker, assure the worker of the three criteria of 'new formality' discussed above, and reach social security to the worker digitally (guaranteed by the state, delivered through private, pubic or hybrid models). Technology can also allow for cross subsidisation of this 'new formal', where the largest beneficiaries of the digital value chain can seed development of such e-governance platforms and innovative bottom of the pyramid social security products. Arguably this is already playing out in telecommunications and broadcasting sectors wherein the cost of infrastructure creation is borne by a very small proportion of end users.

And that's not all. There are many seemingly intractable challenges that enhanced growth of the digital sector and access to technology can resolve that will strengthen economic growth, help with wealth generation and employment. One particularly compelling area is India's characteristically inefficient supply chains. The country's contribution to Global Value Chains (GVCs), both in terms of contribution to forward and backward linkages, is abysmal (Figure 3.1). And so it is not surprising that domestic surveys have repeatedly shown that supply chains are disorganised and a large share of basic inputs are not sourced directly by end users. Similarly, a large share of output is procured by middlemen. The prevalence of agents hinders producers from extracting higher profits and therefore there is a case to be made for harnessing 'digital efficiencies' where possible. A cadre of trained supply chain professionals and supply chain entrepreneurs, empowered with digital technology, can potentially change the way India trades with itself and with the world. This may be particularly important since services account for almost half of value-added in exports globally and this share is higher in developed countries (50%) than in developing countries (38%).

Figure 3.1. **Comparative participation in GVCs, 2009**

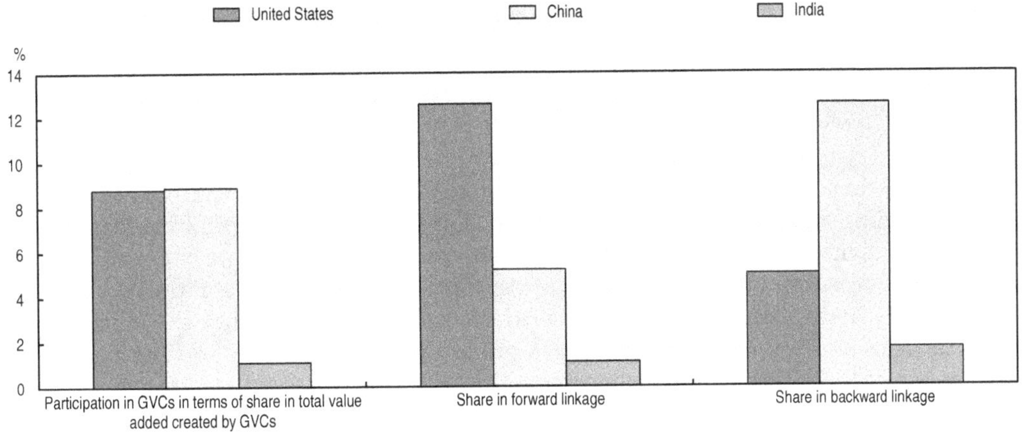

Source: OECD Stat and OECD-WTO TIVA, May 2013.

According to India's telecom regulator, there were around 151 million broadband (above 512 kbps) subscribers (mobile, wired, and wireless subscribers) at the end of April 2016, with a monthly growth in subscriptions of around 5.75% (Telecom Regulatory Authority of India, 2016). Much of this growth in broadband consumption has been driven by smart phone penetration, even at the lower rungs of the economic pyramid. The concomitant proliferation of data services can be harnessed for creating entrepreneurship opportunities and platforms for skill development in areas such as supply chain management. The fact that a large share of India's inward Foreign Direct Investment now comes from technology firms, particularly from the e-commerce and logistics space, bolsters this case.

The role of the public and private sectors

For governments (national and provincial), as well as regulators, the twin goals of promoting affordable digital connectivity while ensuring healthy competition in the market are important. Investments in physical infrastructure are critical to enhancing digital connectivity, and creative partnerships must be pursued to realise them. The emergent digital economy will require a light touch and nimble approach – questions around how the Internet network is built out will have to be answered while balancing interests of a very wide spectrum of stakeholders. Governments will have to keep in mind that policies to govern the digital economy will not only affect economic output, but will also shape the skill development and innovation landscape. The growth in India's services sector, for the most part of the last two decades, has been organic – developed by the knowledge of educated Indians. The digital economy holds the potential to further facilitate the flow of knowledge, and make millions of Indians productive contributors to a 'new formal' workforce.

The private sector's intervention will be no less critical and the effectiveness of India's skill development policy is contingent on robust private-public partnerships. The new government's policy lays thrust on greater policy flexibility to this end. For instance, the nodal body for implementing the policy is open to aligning National Occupational Standards (training standards) with those prevalent in the private sector. There is also a clear emphasis on creating entrepreneurs rather than overburdening the formal job market. And since there is much to be desired in terms of linking skills with market opportunities, the private sector must work with government to create an ecosystem that nurtures start-ups and catalyses self-employment as a viable option. Technology no doubt has a role to play here as well – digital platforms can aid in everything from identification of beneficiaries of skilling programmes to facilitating the visibility of small businesses and in linking availability to demand.

It is also likely that the private sector will play a crucial role in providing, through technological gateways, the "cover" that governments in the past offered to the formal sector – whether it is insurance, healthcare or other forms of financial inclusion. This act of providing formal social cover to the informal sector using digital devices, digital identity and digital last mile, is itself a new growth sector that can create new employment in services. It is important that the government does not regulate these gateways with a heavy hand, even as it grapples with the task of ensuring that they conform to constitutional and international principles around privacy, security and human rights. Since much of the informal and formal sector in the digital space will be transnational in scope, international standards must be embedded within national rules.

If stronger support from the private sector is not forthcoming, the competitiveness of the Indian economy in any sector will be short-lived. It is also a fact that large Indian private sector firms have historically underinvested in their own supply chains and in enhancing the productivity of their workforces. The result has been a significant inability to cope with new regulatory norms or new global standards, and visible under productivity of the economy. Conversely, if India is able to successfully digitise its supply chains, its private sector should also explore whether such digitisation itself is a service that can be exported to other emerging markets in Africa, Asia and Latin America. Additionally, where supply chains are still to be put in place, and technology can assist to leapfrog logistics and supply chain infrastructure obstacles faced by local industry, the Indian experience and Indian corporations can become solution providers to GVCs when positioned alongside the unfolding and essential Indian engagement with skill development, entrepreneurship and informality.

Section 4. The uncertain emergence of MENA 3.0
Hussein Al-Majali[5]

The Middle East and North Africa (MENA) region today is grappling with unprecedented volatility and change. The butterfly effect of a young Tunisian fruit seller assaulted by a government official in December 2010 has turned what initially held up the hope of an Arab Spring into a long and violent Arab Winter.

As of early 2017 there is no sign of the long winter coming to an end. Conflict still rages across Iraq, the Syrian Arab Republic, Yemen and Libya, and terrorism remains a constant threat everywhere. The structural drivers of the Israeli-Palestinian conflict remain unresolved and much of Gaza Strip is in ruin. Austerity measures introduced across much of the region due to the protracted global downturn in oil prices, including the wealthier and largely conflict-free Gulf Co-operation Council (GCC) economies, are having a biting effect on household income levels and broader measures of wellbeing and life satisfaction.

While it is not clear when, or indeed how, the region's multiple conflicts will be de-escalated to the extent that hostilities stop between warring parties, it is clear that the next 15 years will be a critical inflection point for the region.

To appreciate the importance of this inflection point it is worth looking backwards over the past century.

One-hundred years ago during World War I and its immediate aftermath, the political economy of the modern MENA region was predominantly shaped by colonial administration and tribal tradition. Fifty years ago most of the region had migrated to new republican or monarchical governance models characterised by state paternalism. Fifty years on, the region today is experiencing the messy, and all too often violent, process of forging yet another model of political economy.

How 'MENA 3.0' turns out is very much in play. The next 15 years will be critical and the contours of the political economy that emerges will have global implications. It is too early to foresee what MENA 3.0 will look like, but a number of key drivers of this new regional political economy are worth highlighting.

First, while one single new model of political economy will not prevail over the entire MENA region, the way in which the Arab Spring movement swept through the region highlights the power of memes across the Arab world. Arabs from the Maghreb to the Levant feel a strong sense of common cause. As improvisation and innovation in political economy occurs in one part of the region, it will influence action and reaction elsewhere in the region as it has in the past.

Unfortunately, we have seen the toxic, violent extremist versions of these memes spread dangerously in the past few years. Progressive government and civil society leaders, supported by the international community, must come together to counter these toxic memes by creating positive and scalable citizen-centric models of political economy that can be part of re-establishing law, order and security across the region as a basis for rebuilding the prosperity of families and communities.

Second, it is the generation aged between 15-30 years old today who will determine how MENA 3.0 evolves. They represent around 30% of the region's population and their rapid uptake of technology and social media over the past decade has led to attitudes, beliefs and expectations that are radically different from those of their parents and grandparents. Through social media they have a voice unlike any generation in the MENA region over the past century. That expression, in all its various forms, is fundamentally challenging the prevailing governance model of state paternalism.

The critical and urgent challenge today is to channel the energy of Arab youth into what His Majesty King Abdullah II of Jordan has called 'active citizenship'. Only by finding productive and civic-minded pathways for their voice and talents can we avoid the alternatives: apathy or radicalization.

Third, active citizenship must be underwritten by meaningful employment. Across the region, youth unemployment is commonly cited as being around 30%; but that understates the calcification of the problem and the broader crisis of employability. Labour market reform in this context is not just an economic development imperative but a national security one.

The challenge is immense and multi-faceted. Across the MENA region, family expectations need to be reshaped to value all types of vocational employment – not just engineers and doctors. Private sector leaders need to commit to training and mentoring their own youth rather than importing cheap foreign labour. Governments need to embrace bolder policy initiatives and regulatory incentives to break through the deeply structural nature of the barriers to workforce participation.

Governments must also open up greater space for innovative new solutions to the challenge of delivering high quality STEM education and vocational training. There is also an urgent need to improve the matching of demand and supply across the labour market. International experience has shown that innovation can come from both the private sector and civil society organisations. There is greater need for innovation in policy, service delivery and public finance than ever before given the current pressure of budget austerity. Private sector and civil society solutions can and should be facilitated through innovative new financing mechanisms such as social impact bonds that help take proven interventions to scale.

Fourth, a new regional conflict resolution architecture is a pre-requisite for development. Leaders across the MENA region today are overwhelmed with their national security agenda. We cannot hope to elevate issues of development and prosperity on the national leadership agenda until the various conflicts across the region are taken off the battlefield and quarantined through effective multilateral diplomacy.

Fifth, as the international community weighs up its choices about where and how to support a process of transformation in the MENA region, it is important to emphasise that this is not a uniform struggle over whether or not to embrace the modalities of western liberal democracy. Whether or not the global economy is about to enter a new period of protectionism, today's Arab citizens have much the same wellbeing expectations as their counterparts around the world. What the region is going through now is a much deeper process of redefining the relationship between citizen and state in a modern global economy.

The international community has a critical role to play in supporting and underwriting the process of reimagining and redeveloping the conflict-affected parts of the MENA region. Policy makers, the private sector and civil society leaders will benefit from the reinforcement of principles and standards of excellence. Governments will require policy advice, regulatory design support and capability building. Rapid prototyping and scaling of solutions customised to local environments, not blanket prescriptions, will be the key to success.

In this respect, the Gulf States and in particular the Emirates of Dubai and Abu Dhabi as well as Bahrain and Doha have a unique and vital role to play. As the region's least conflict-affected economies and most advanced and globally connected cities they have the opportunity over the next 15 years to play the role of both conduit and catalyst for the human capital and financial capital that needs to be marshalled for the challenges ahead.

It is not immediately apparent through the fog of war and conflict engulfing the region today, but a broader process of social, economic and political transformation is underway. Unfortunately but perhaps unsurprisingly, that process is neither linear nor peaceful. The international community has a lot at stake in how 'MENA 3.0' emerges and a lot to contribute to help steer that process towards comprehensive security and inclusive development for all citizens of the region.

Notes

1. René N'Guettia Kouassi (Ph.D) is Director of the Economic Affairs Department of the African Union Commission.

2. Gilbert Houngbo is the Deputy Director-General of the International Labour Organisation (since March 2013), leading the Organisation's field operations in more than 100 countries as well as its bilateral and multilateral partnerships.

3. Samir Saran (Ph.D) leads the Observer Research Foundation's (ORF) outreach and business development activities, and heads the ORF Global Governance and Cyber and Media programmes in India.

4. Vivan Sharan leads Koan Advisory's macro-advisory and regulatory practice in New Delhi.

5. Hussein Al-Majali is Executive Vice Chairman, Middle East and North Africa at Magellan Global Advisers.

References

ILO (2015a), "The future of work centenary initiative", *Report of the Director-General*, Report I, International Labour Conference, 104th Session, 2015. http://www.ilo.org/wcmsp5/groups/public/@ed_norm/@relconf/documents/meetingdocument/wcms_369026.pdf.

ILO (2015b), "Global Employment Trends for Youth 2015: Scaling up investments in decent jobs for youth", International Labour Organisation, Geneva, http://www.ilo.org/wcmsp5/groups/public/---dgreports/---dcomm/---publ/documents/publication/wcms_412015.pdf.

ILO (2015c), "What works for youth employment? Innovative experiences in the transition to formality: An Initiative under the ILO's Area of Critical Importance on Jobs and Skills for Youth (ACI 2)", Lima, 22-24 April, 2015, http://www.ilo.org/wcmsp5/groups/public/---ed_emp/---ed_emp_msu/documents/meetingdocument/wcms_381171.pdf.

ILO (2015d), "Promoting Formal Employment Among Youth: Innovative Experiences in Latin America and the Caribbean", ILO Regional Office for Latin America and the Caribbean, Lima, http://www.ilo.org/wcmsp5/groups/public/---americas/---ro-lima/documents/publication/wcms_361990.pdf.

ILO (2014a), *Thematic Labour Overview. Transition to Formality in Latin America and the Caribbean.* ILO Regional Office for Latin America and the Caribbean, Lima, http://www.ilo.org/wcmsp5/groups/public/---americas/---ro-lima/documents/publication/wcms_314469.pdf.

ILO (2014b), "Transitioning from the informal to the formal economy", Report V (1), and Report V (2), *International Labour Conference*, 103rd session, Geneva. International Labour Conference, http://www.ilo.org/wcmsp5/groups/public/---ed_norm/---relconf/documents/meetingdocument/wcms_218128.pdf.

ILO (2013), *Trabajo Decente y Juventud en América Latina. Políticas para la acción,* Regional Office for Latin America and the Caribbean, Lima, http://www.ilo.org/wcmsp5/groups/public/---americas/---ro-lima/documents/publication/wcms_235577.pdf.

ILO (2012), "The youth employment crisis: A call for action", Resolution and conclusions of the 101st Session of the International Labour Conference, Geneva, 2012, https://www.dol.gov/ilab/reports/pdf/ILC%20Committee%20on%20Youth%20Employment%20Crisis.pdf

Observer Research Foundation (2013), *68th Round, National Sample Survey,* India Data Labs, Observer Research Foundation, New Delhi.

OECD (2016), *OECD Stat and OECD-WTO TiVA, May 2013,* http://stats.oecd.org/

Shehu, E. and Nilsson, B. (2014), "Informal employment among youth: Evidence from 20 school-to-work transition surveys", *Work4Youth Publication Series No. 8,* International Labour Office, Geneva, http://www.ilo.org/wcmsp5/groups/public/@dgreports/@dcomm/documents/publication/wcms_234911.pdf.

Telecom Regulatory Authority of India (2016), *Press Release no. 49/2016,* TRAI, New Delhi, http://www.trai.gov.in/sites/default/files/Press_Release_No.49_20_june_2016_Eng_0.pdf.

UNDP (2013), *Humanity Divided: Confronting Inequality in Developing Countries,* UNDP Bureau for Development Policy, New York, http://www.undp.org/content/dam/undp/library/Poverty%20Reduction/Inclusive%20development/Humanity%20Divided/HumanityDivided_Full-Report.pdf.

UNRISD (2012), "Inequalities and the Post-2015 Development Agenda", *Research and Policy Brief 15,* October 2012, , UNRISD, Geneva, http://www.unrisd.org/80256B3C005BCCF9/(httpAuxPages)/F7619CAD1B60C5D3C1257A8C0035A481/$file/RPB15e.pdf.

Chapter 4

The low-carbon transition challenge in ASEAN countries and the BRICS

Chapter 4 analyses some of the crucial energy and environmental risks and challenges developing and emerging countries face over the coming 15 years. Developing and emerging countries both suffer the disproportional burden of the negative effects of climate change and are experiencing rapid increases in energy demands as their populations grow and urbanise. Sanjayan Velautham discusses the ASEAN community's "energy trilemma": the trade-off between energy security, environmental sustainability and economic competitiveness. Tian Huifang writes about the obstacles facing the BRICS as they attempt to transition to low-carbon economies and how they can spur global co-operation on mitigating climate change.

Chapter 4 explores some of the crucial energy and environmental challenges developing countries face over the coming 15 years. The overview chapter highlighted rapid population growth and urbanisation occurring in several developing regions, particularly sub-Saharan Africa and South Asia. These two trends will contribute to developing countries' increasing demand for energy over the coming decades. Moreover, the negative effects of climate change disproportionately fall on poorer regions, contributing to higher mortality rates due to climate shocks, the loss of arable land due to desertification, biodiversity loss, forced migration, water scarcity, and increased competition over resources.

The authors of the sections in this Chapter write about the transition to low-carbon economies in this context of growing energy demands and environmental degradation. Sanjayan Velautham outlines the ASEAN community's "energy trilemma": negotiating the trade-offs between energy security, environmental sustainability and economic competitiveness. Velautham proposes two key policy areas to help manage the trilemma: energy efficiency and conservation (EE&C) and diversifying energy options. EE&C can contribute to economic savings, energy security and climate change mitigation. The deployment of renewable energy sources currently is challenged by a variety of factors, including perceived high production costs, inadequate regulatory measures, complex and time-consuming permit procedures, and grid compatibility. Velautham is encouraged by the collective agreement by member countries on the ASEAN Plan of Action for Energy Co-operation 2016-2025 to develop and adopt a regional Renewable Energy Roadmap by 2020.

In a different vein, Tian Huifang analyses the major risks and challenges facing the BRICS as they attempt to transition to low-carbon economies. Tian notes that all the BRICS exhibit high levels of energy consumption, emissions and heavy pollution. In addition, they are threatened by a variety of climate-related vulnerabilities, including rainforest biodiversity in Brazil, agricultural productivity in India and China, and water scarcity in South Africa. Tian further outlines several significant obstacles to the BRICS' green transformation, such as competitiveness barriers from the use of traditional fossil fuels in current markets, an inadequate legal and regulatory framework to stimulate the use of renewable energy, the lack of necessary infrastructure for the development of the green economy, and inadequate levels of green and climate financing. She proposes a five-pronged policy agenda to accelerate this transformation: push the G20 on climate governance and the commitment to mobilise USD 100 billion per year by 2020 to support climate adaptation and mitigation in developing countries; develop climate mitigation policies to incentivise the private sector to shift investment toward renewables; change the structure of energy production; integrate green finance into national development strategies; and align broader policies and regulations with decarbonisation goals.

Together, the sections in this Chapter analyse some of the most pressing global environmental risks and challenges facing developing countries over the next 15 years. The contributions to this Chapter neither represent the positions of the Development Centre nor the OECD, but are solely the authors' own views.

Section 1. Addressing energy challenges in the rise of the ASEAN economic community
Sanjayan Velautham[1]

ASEAN is considered one of the fastest growing regions in the world. In 2016, ASEAN continued to hold its position as the third largest economy in Asia and the seventh largest in the world. As the growth is expected to continue, a reliable, accessible, and sustainable supply of energy will be essential. Like countries and regions around the world, ASEAN faces the challenge of overcoming what is called the "energy trilemma"; finding the right balance between energy security, environmental sustainability and economic competitiveness. The ASEAN Economic Community (AEC) framework launched in 2015 creates opportunities for advancing energy efficiency, deploying renewable and alternative energy, and ensuring individual and regional energy security.

Growing economy calls for energy efficiency

To achieve sustainability in the energy sector, ASEAN continued to focus on energy efficiency and renewable energy as the 'twin pillars' of sustainable energy policy. Both resources must be developed aggressively to enhance energy security and reduce the environmental impact of energy use in the region. Energy efficiency and conservation is viewed as one of the most effective ways to meet the growing demand in terms of energy supply security and to reduce the environmental impacts of development. Energy efficiency and conservation can contribute to economic savings, energy security and climate change mitigation. ASEAN has put forward several measures to improve efficiency at all stages of the energy chain (Table 4.1). The region is aiming for a 20% energy intensity reduction by 2020 based on the year 2005 level.

Table 4.1. **ASEAN member states' energy efficiency potential**

Member State	Energy Efficiency Potential	Reference Document
Brunei Darussalam	Brunei Darussalam's target is to reduce energy intensity by 45% by 2035 in line with the country's commitment to the Asia-Pacific Economic Cooperation through supply and demand side measures.	The Energy White Paper 2014
Cambodia	The energy efficiency in Cambodia is applied similarly for all sectors, with target of 15% reduction in 2035. Total energy saving in Cambodia by that year would be about 1 Mtoe.	National Policy, Strategy and Action Plan on Energy Efficiency (2016)
Indonesia	1% reduction on energy intensity reduction per year until 2025.	National Energy Efficiency Master Plan (RIKEN) 2014
Lao PDR	10 % energy saving from Business as Usual (BaU) by 2030.	National Policy on Energy Efficiency and Conservation.
Malaysia	8% reduction from BaU on electricity demand until 2030.	National Energy Efficiency Action Plan (NEEAP) 2016-2025
Myanmar	12% reduction on energy consumption by 2020, baseline 2020.	The Energy Efficiency and Conservation Policy, Strategy and Roadmap (EECPSR)
The Philippines	40% energy intensity reduction in 2040, Baseline 2010.	Energy Efficiency Roadmap for the Philippines 2017-2040
Singapore	35% energy intensity improvement in 2036, baseline 2010.	Singapore Sustainable Blueprint (SSB)
Thailand	30% energy intensity reduction in 2036 compared to that in 2010.	Energy Efficiency Development Plan (EEP) 2015
Viet Nam	5% reduction from BaU on Energy Consumption 2016-2020.	EE&C National Target Programme 2016-2020

Source: Author's compilation.

Some barriers to energy efficiency implementation have been observed to be similar in ASEAN member states, such as: i) high energy subsidies become a hindrance for the industries and companies trying to implement energy efficiency measures through business models; ii) the lack of a regulatory framework and robust policies; iii) the absence of an appropriate institutional mechanism to provide long-term support for energy efficiency implementation; iv) the lack of financial support to intensify high capital investment for smaller companies to undertake energy efficiency measures; and v) the lack of standards and infrastructure to test the energy performances of appliances and equipment. To some extent, some ASEAN member states have been looking at gradually phasing out the energy subsidies to encourage investments in energy efficiency.

To pursue the regional energy efficiency target, ASEAN is implementing outcome-based strategies set in the *ASEAN Plan of Action for Energy Co-operation (APAEC) 2016-2025* (ASEAN Centre for Energy, 2015a) for energy efficiency and conservation: i) harmonisation and promotion of energy efficiency standards and labelling on various kinds of energy-related products; ii) enhancing private sector participation, including energy service companies, for energy efficiency and conservation promotion; iii) developing green building codes which support the use of high energy efficient products; iv) enhancing the participation of financial institutions in energy efficiency and conservation development. Moreover, most ASEAN member states should concentrate on enacting a wide range of legislation and regulations for energy conservation and environmental protection. Awareness-raising needs to be increased among the public and economy sectors.

An example of activities taken under the framework of Strategy 1 (on energy efficiency standards and labelling) is implemented within the co-operation of ASEAN+3 (ASEAN + China, Japan, Korea) Mitigation Programme 2016. Under this programme, the ASEAN Centre for Energy (ACE) and the ASEAN member states have been conducting the consultative process on policy and testing procedure of energy efficiency standards and labelling for refrigerators in Cambodia, among others.

Diversifying energy options

The promising growth of the AEC calls for more energy sources to reduce the region's dependence on fossil fuels. According to the *APAEC 2016-2025* (Ibid.), the aspirational target to increase the component of renewable energy to 23% by 2025 in ASEAN energy mix provides an opportunity to accelerate renewable energy deployment in the region with larger investment and with the development of more affordable and reliable technologies.

ASEAN is going towards the right direction to boost renewable energy development in the region. The share of renewables in Total Primary Energy Supply (TPES) in 2015 is around 10%; a significant increase from 1990 with compound annual growth rate of 8% (Figure 4.1). Meanwhile in the power sector (Figure 4.2), the deployment of renewable energy in the last 8 years has doubled with total installed capacity of around 57 GW in 2015. The compound annual growth rate of overall renewables in the power sector is around 10%, while that of fossil fuels is only 5.6%. The growth is even more promising for variable renewable energy, i.e. wind and solar PV, with a compound annual growth rate of 45% and 62% respectively. This trend seems to continue in the upcoming years, which means that renewables will play a bigger role in ASEAN.

However, despite this remarkable growth, there is still a lack of local technical capacity in project development in some member states, and not all financial institutions are familiar with the risks of renewable energy which causes the reluctance to finance renewable energy projects. These challenges also provide opportunities to raise the awareness of the financial sector and to build the region's capacity. The latter could be done with regional and/or international co-operation. ACE plans that collaboration with ASEAN's Dialogue Partners, International Organisations, academic institutions and the business sector will be stepped up to benefit from their expertise and to enhance capacity building in the region. One example is through co-operation with Deutsche Gesellschaft für Internationale Zusammenarbeit (GIZ) GmbH on behalf of the Federal Ministry for Economic Co-operation and Development (BMZ). Focus group discussions, training and capacity building activities, joint studies and information dissemination were conducted to help shape influential renewable energy policies and increase the deployment of renewable energy projects in the ASEAN member states. Such activities include: i) greater role of renewable energy in ASEAN power sector; ii) impacts of renewable energy integration through grid connection; iii) renewable energy lending guidelines; iv) training for trainers for renewable energy training institutions; v) standardised cost of electricity of renewable energy (ASEAN Centre for Energy, 2016b) and vi) renewable energy permit procedures guidelines and recommendation (ASEAN Centre for Energy, 2016c).

Figure 4.1. Renewable energy share in total primary energy supply

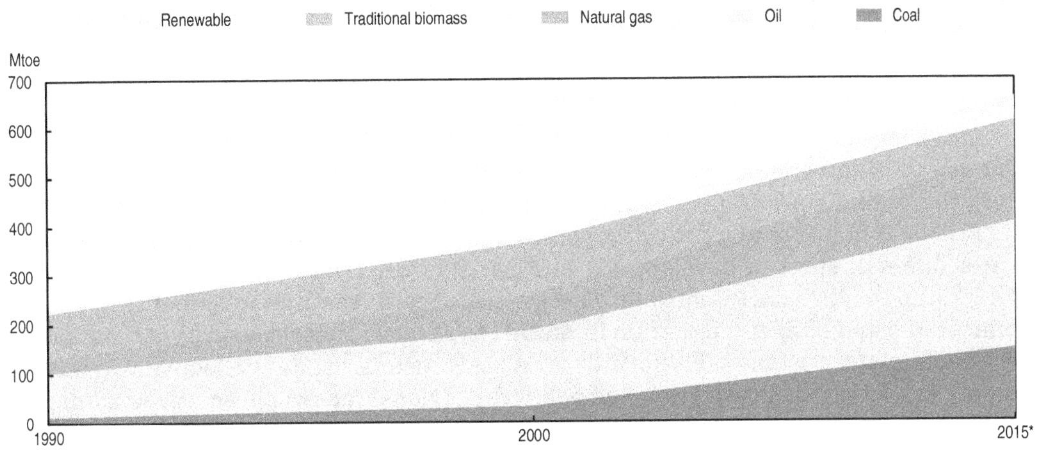

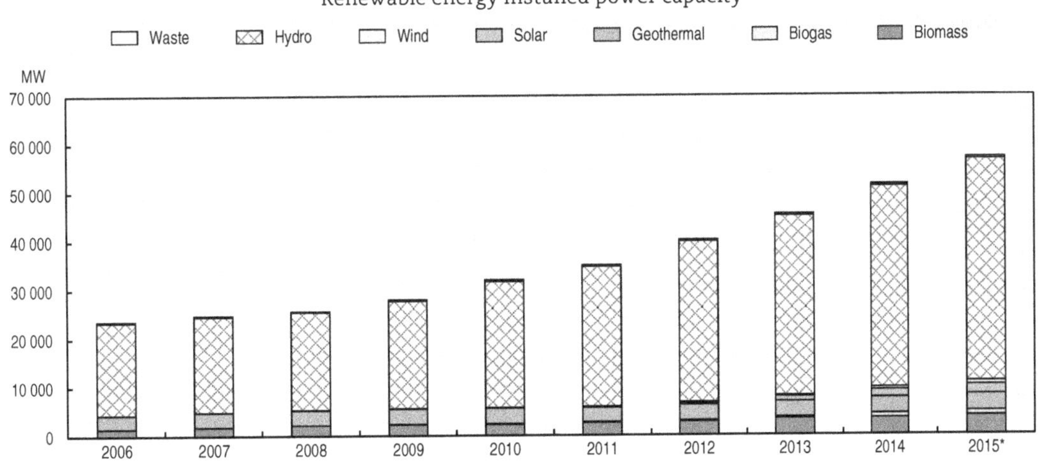

Note: *Denotes unofficial preliminary data, based on projections.
Source: Author's calculations based on ASEAN Centre for Energy (2016a), ASEAN Centre for Energy Database.

Figure 4.2. Renewable energy development in the power sector
Renewable energy installed power capacity

Note: *Denotes unofficial preliminary data, based on projection
Source: Author's calculations based on ASEAN Centre for Energy (2016a), ASEAN Centre for Energy Database.

As renewable energy deployment's main challenges in ASEAN are i) perceived high production costs; ii) inadequate renewable energy policy and regulatory measures; as well as iii) complex and time-consuming permit procedures, there is ample opportunity for policy co-ordination between ASEAN member states to reduce production costs, as indicated by the data and analysis of one of ACE's publications, the *4th ASEAN Energy Outlook* (ASEAN Centre for Energy, 2015b). Appropriate feed-in tariffs, simplified permit procedures, attractive incentives, and financing support mechanisms can be policy tools to encourage the growth of renewables in ASEAN. Bold and robust incentives will need to be considered to drive a cleaner and more sustainable energy infrastructure to power the region's economic growth going forward. Other challenges for renewable energy in ASEAN include grids compatibility and distance to be connected to renewable energy sources. On-grid connection of variable renewable energy sources needs to be solved in a comprehensive way. The utilities companies could combine variable renewable energy sources with flexible back-up power plants that provide reliable energy storage technologies, reliable forecasting, and demand-side energy management. For the challenge of grids' distance from the source, distributed connection could be one of the solutions. Apart from optimising renewable energy potential in remote areas, such solution could increase electricity access in remote or rural areas.

According to the ACE and the International Renewable Energy Agency (IRENA)'s latest joint report, *Renewable Energy Outlook for ASEAN* (IRENA and ASEAN Centre for Energy, 2016), there is no single set of solutions suited to the needs of the entire ASEAN region. The ACE does not offer any policy proposals to the region as each ASEAN member state is at a different stage of development and has its own priorities. However, under the APAEC 2016-2025 (ASEAN Centre for Energy, 2015a) with the theme 'Enhancing Energy Connectivity and Market Integration in ASEAN to Achieve Energy Security, Accessibility, Affordability and Sustainability for All', all ASEAN member states collectively agreed to execute the action plan to develop and adopt the regional renewable energy Roadmap by 2020.

Section 2. Gathering momentum for climate co-operation: from the perspective of the BRICS
Tian Huifang[2]

Opportunity

In current world, two transformations are likely to dominate the first half of the twenty-first century. The first is the shift in economic power from the West to the East with the group rise of emerging economics, especially the BRICS (Brazil, the Russian Federation, India, China and South Africa) countries. Globally and politically, the influence of the BRICS is rapidly increasing. The second is the transition from a high to low carbon economy. The average temperature has been gradually increasing throughout the entire world. Global warming is recognised as the most important risk factor that threatens the very existence and advancement of humanity. Stern (2007) famously called climate change the greatest market failure of all time. Combining growth patterns and sustainability in terms of economic, social and ecological development is a key challenge for any nation.

The urgency of the crisis gives governments of the developing nations the chance to redirect resources to more efficient economic growth that is better for the environment, more socially equitable, and more promising over the long term, by promoting growth in relevant sectors – including energy efficiency, sustainable agriculture and off-grid renewable power. How can economic growth be shaped in a sustainable way? An increasing number of countries are elaborating national strategies for sustainable development that base economic growth on a long-term foundation, balancing the interests of the economy, society and the environment. It may not automatically solve the current poverty and climate imperatives. It will however, provide multiple social, economic and environmental dividends and constitute much-needed first steps towards low-carbon social and economic development.

In the process of defining such strategies, the visions and practical experiences of countries such as the BRICS countries regarding sustainable development are of crucial global importance. A marked shift from the 1992 Rio Earth Summit to the 2012 Rio+20 Summit has been the role of emerging economies. Although the five countries have different economic endowments, they are facing similar challenges to sustain economic growth, save natural resources, and protect the environment. BRICS countries' co-operation provides a platform to share experiences and tackle challenges as they have different competitive advantages and their economies are highly complementary. Reflecting the broadening of the BRICS agenda since the first BRICS summit was held in 2009, the first ever meeting of BRICS environment ministers was held in the Russian Federation in April 2015. The ministers agreed to:

- establish a working group on environment to identify priority areas of co-operation;
- explore the potential of the BRICS New Development Bank (NDB) to fund environmental projects;
- explore the possibility of establishing a collaborative platform of the BRICS countries to share best environmental practices and facilitate the exchange of environmentally sound technologies and know-how with participation of public and private stakeholders;
- identify the need to establish a public-private partnership mechanism to increase green investments. Establishing a platform for sharing green technologies has been endorsed at the 7th BRICS summit in the Russian city of Ufa in 2015.

Challenges

From the national level, all BRICS have to face the problems of high energy consumption, high emissions and heavy pollution. Moreover, all countries are vulnerable to climate change. As a country rich in biodiversity and vast tropical forests, Brazil is vulnerable to climate change due to its fragile, biologically diverse ecosystems. The impact of global warming is increasingly apparent in the Russian Federation, which is causing rare extreme heat and dry weather. About half of the Indian population is dependent on agriculture or other climate sensitive sectors. Climate change has already produced visible adverse effects on China's agriculture and livestock-raising sectors, manifested by increased instability in agricultural production, severe damages to crops and livestock breeding caused by floods, drought and high temperatures in some parts of the country. Climate change also poses a significant threat to South Africa's water resources, food security, health, infrastructure, as well as its ecosystem services and biodiversity. BRICS have to improve their ability to mitigate climate change through internal co-operation, and also express the appeal in the same voice to set up a fair and reasonable global climate governance regime.

Further, many barriers must be overcome to make BRICS' green transformation financially viable. These barriers include:

- competitiveness barriers from the use of traditional fossil fuels in the current market environment;
- institutional and regulatory barriers due to the lack of a legal and regulatory framework to stimulate the use of renewable energy;
- the lack of the necessary infrastructure for the successful development of the green economy;
- the inadequate level and quality of climate-friendly technology support;
- the inadequate level of green financing and climate finance;
- inadequate human resources and the lack of appropriate data about carbon emissions.

Policy proposals and solutions

The BRICS summits and related actions provide a platform to share experiences and deal with the common challenge of climate change. Deepening future climate co-operation and promoting BRICS economy transformation is obviously significant. I propose the following areas to enhance BRICS' co-operation on climate change:

First of all, being deeply involved in global climate governance, by pushing G20 members to take effective actions in response to climate change, following through on the Paris Agreement, and by pushing developed countries to meet the commitment to mobilise USD 100 billion per year by 2020 to support climate adaptation and mitigation in developing countries and providing additional sources for climate finance. Meanwhile, as stipulated in the Paris Agreement, BRICS governments – along with every government – need to formulate at the earliest possible date their national long-term low carbon emissions development strategies, and regularly renew their ambition for nationally determined contributions (NDCs). For this, a formal co-operation mechanism on climate change can be set up, for example, the BRICS climate working group can work closely with the BRICS energy working group and agriculture working group, enhance the dialogue with south and north countries, and work closely with the G20 development working group and climate change study group to promote the implementation of the Paris Agreement nationally and globally.

Second, strong and coherent climate mitigation policies are needed to incentivise the private sector to shift investment away from fossil-fuel-based technologies towards Renewable Energy Sources (RESs). Such policies should include explicit carbon pricing (e.g. carbon taxes and emissions trading), targeted investment incentives (e.g. feed-in tariffs and public tenders), reform of inefficient fossil-fuel subsidies; and targeted support of innovation, e.g. through public R&D expenditures.

Third, energy structure transformation and energy security are critical for the shared prosperity of humanity and for the future of the planet. Overall energy consumption shall be managed by gradually phasing out fossil fuel subsidies and increasing the share of renewables in the energy mix and higher global energy efficiency. The imperative of affordable, clean and renewable energy access to all should be acknowledged. Moreover, the recent evolution of financing structures, along with substantial policy support to RESs has boosted increased investment in renewable projects and contributed to decreasing technology costs. Global new investment in renewable energy has reached an all-time record of USD 286 billion in 2015, with a shift in geographic deployment towards Asia (FS-UNEP Collaborating Centre, 2016). Policies need to specifically target the risks associated with the deployment of renewables and find a smart way to remove or mitigate them.

Fourth, green finance shall be integrated into national development strategies. Active efforts should be made to deliver green financial products and services, channel public funds and social capital into green projects, promote green PPP projects and increase investment in nature. Green taxation shall be taken into consideration and green bonds can be introduced to allow financial institutions to raise funds for green projects. In carrying out domestic and international economic projects, impacts on the environmental and social dimensions shall be taken into account and be assessed. Laws and regulations shall be formulated to enforce financial institutions and enterprises to disclose information on environmental and social impacts and protect the public's rights to know and supervise. It is also necessary to establish a public-private partnership mechanism to increase private green investments. Green and low-carbon cities, green designs, green supply chain, green infrastructure, green consumption, green families and green traveling shall be promoted and green education shall be included in school curriculums.

Fifth, broader policies and regulations should be aligned with decarbonisation goals in order to create a supportive and green investment environment for low-carbon investment. Governments and regulators should take a more regional and holistic approaches to electricity network planning domestically and cross-border, public financial institutions such as multilateral development banks can play an active role in addressing obstacles encountered by projects, ranging from overseeing the compliance on permit granting procedures, to facilitating access to finance. For example, the BRICS New Development Bank can provide long-term and low-cost financing support. A green fund under the BRICS Bank can be set up to finance green projects and assist in the deployment of green technologies. The BRICS New Development Bank itself should be green, which means it should pay more attention to local environment conservation and biodiversity protection in its financial activities.

Last but most importantly, co-operation will require the help of political trust, the help of institutional innovation, the help of investment and trade facilitation, technology transfer mechanisms, and above all, societies willing to change the current development pattern for future social benefit and environmental quality.

Notes

1. Sanjayan Velautham (Ph.D) is Executive Director of the ASEAN Centre for Energy.
2. Tian Huifang (Ph.D) is the Deputy Director and Senior Research Fellow at the Department of Global Governance at the Institute of World Economics and Politics, Chinese Academy of Social Sciences (CASS) in Beijing.

References

ASEAN Centre for Energy (2016a), *ASEAN Centre for Energy Database*, http://aeds.aseanenergy.org/.

ASEAN Centre for Energy (2016b), "Levelised Cost of Electricity of Selected Renewable Technologies in the ASEAN Member States", Jakarta, http://www.aseanenergy.org/resources/publications/asean-resp-levelised-cost-of-electricity-of-selected-renewable-technologies-in-the-asean-member-states/.

ASEAN Centre for Energy (2016c), "Solar Photovoltaic (Small) Project Development in Malaysia", *Renewable Energy Guideline*, ASEAN Centre for Energy, Jakarta, http://www.aseanenergy.org/resources/asean-resp-re-guideline-on-solar-photovoltaic-small-project-development-in-malaysia/.

ASEAN Centre for Energy (2015a), "ASEAN Plan of Action for Energy Co-operation (APAEC) 2016 – 2025", 33rd Ministers on Energy Meeting, Kuala Lumpur, Malaysia, October 2015, http://www.aseanenergy.org/resources/publications/asean-plan-of-action-for-energy-cooperation-apaec-2016-2025/.

ASEAN Centre for Energy (2015b), *The 4th ASEAN Energy Outlook*, Jakarta, http://www.aseanenergy.org/resources/publications/the-4th-asean-energy-outlook/.

IRENA and ASEAN Centre for Energy (2016), *Renewable Energy Outlook for ASEAN: a REmap Analysis*, International Renewable Energy Agency (IRENA), Abu Dhabi and ASEAN Centre for Energy (ACE), Jakarta, http://www.aseanenergy.org/resources/publications/renewable-energy-outlook-for-asean-a-remap-analysis/.

FS-UNEP Collaborating Centre (2016), *Global Trends in Renewable Energy Investment 2016*, Frankfurt School-UNEP Centre, Frankfurt am Main, http://fs-unep-centre.org/sites/default/files/publications/globaltrendsinrenewableenergyinvestment2016lowres_0.pdf.

Stern, N. (2007), *The Economics of Climate Change. The Stern Review*, Cambridge University Press, Cambridge.

Chapter 5

New forms of development co-operation

Chapter 5 is concerned with new and improved forms of development co-operation at a time when the concept of development itself is in transition. The universal SDGs agenda make it apparent that aid is no longer sufficient to achieve shared development goals; this point is made more pertinent as countries graduate from ODA eligibility – development goes beyond income thresholds. Debapriya Bhattacharya and Sarah Sabin Khan argue that the LDCs represent a key "battleground" for the implementation of the SDGs agenda and outline three policy areas on which the international community could focus to prevent them from being left behind. Andrea Vignolo and Karen Van Rompaey write about the need for new forms of development co-operation as countries graduate from ODA eligibility.

The realisation that aid alone is insufficient to achieve shared development goals, and the recognition of an increasingly complex development architecture, have contributed to the drive for new forms of development co-operation articulated in the Sustainable Development Goals. Development co-operation will take on a greater variety of forms and be delivered by a broader array of stakeholders, including the private sector and foundations. This is particularly important given the shift to a more constrained economic climate for developing countries, as the overview chapter outlined. This is matched by a more volatile global financial system making international finance increasingly difficult for developing countries to access. Furthermore, as countries graduate from Official Development Assistance (ODA) eligibility, it becomes increasingly clear that development co-operation will have to be about more than aid. The authors of the following chapters explore some of the themes associated with development co-operation in more detail.

Debapriya Bhattacharya and Sarah Sabin Khan highlight the importance of least developed countries (LDCs) as a key "battleground" for the implementation of the 2030 Agenda. Few LDCs have graduated from the group since the introduction of the LDC category in 1971: only four countries have graduated since 1994. They face a number of key challenges over the coming 15 years including: slowing economic convergence with the advanced countries, inequality and jobless growth, lack of economic diversification, dependency on natural resources, high preponderance of conflict situations, and vulnerability to economic and climactic shocks. To mitigate the risk of the LDCs being left behind in light of these challenges, the authors argue three key policy perspectives could be considered: increased financial resources, access to technology and support for capacity building from the international community; enhanced protection from various systemic risks; and enabling domestic reforms to complement international support measures.

Andrea Vignolo and Karen Van Rompaey stress the need for new forms of development co-operation as countries graduate from ODA eligibility. Enhancing domestic resource mobilisation and continuing to promote South-South and triangular co-operation are two important planks in this recalibrated vision of development co-operation. ODA will continue to play a role in development co-operation but graduation criteria should be broadened to include other multi-dimensional measures of well-being and sustainability beyond GNI and an alternative timeframe, according to the universality of the 2030 Agenda.

The sections in this chapter provide a useful primer for thinking about how development co-operation may evolve in the future and provide a fitting conclusion to the anthology. The contributions to this chapter neither represent the positions of the Development Centre nor the OECD, but are solely the authors' own views.

Section 1. Will the least developed countries be left behind? The risks of a universal development agenda

Debapriya Bhattacharya[1] and Sarah Sabin Khan[2]

The 2030 Agenda for Sustainable Development was unanimously adopted by 193 heads of state and government at the United Nations General Assembly in September 2015. The signatories made an expressed commitment to "leave no one behind" in their efforts to achieve the Sustainable Development Goals (SDGs) outlined in the agenda. This inclusive development agenda will begin with the least developed countries (LDCs) – the poorest and most vulnerable among developing countries. They will likely emerge as the "battleground" for implementation of the 2030 Agenda (UNCTAD, 2015). The LDCs remain largely marginalised, even 45 years after the introduction of the LDC category in 1971 with a view to highlight their plight and attract special international support. Out of the 48 countries currently categorised as LDCs, almost half also fall under another recognised vulnerability category. The LDCs include 17 landlocked developing countries, nine small island developing states and 24 conflict-affected or post-conflict countries. As a group, the LDCs are also extremely vulnerable to climate change owing to their relatively limited capacity to mitigate its impacts.

Going forward, the progress of the LDCs should be one of the metrics for progress against the commitment to leave no one behind. Globally, the number of people living below the extreme poverty line (below USD 1.9 per day at 2011 Purchasing Power Parity)[3] decreased in absolute terms from an estimated average of 1.9 billion in the 1980s to an estimated average of 1.1 billion in the 2000s, a trend that translated into a remarkable decrease in the share of the global population living in poverty from 40% to 16.7%. In contrast, the poor increased both in number as well as a percentage of the global poor within the LDCs. Compared to the growing share of the LDC population in the global population from an average of 9% to 12%, the LDC share of the global poor increased at a rather fast pace from approximately 15.7% to 33.6% between the 1980s and 2000s. With 31% of the global poor residing among only 12% of the global population in LDCs, SDG 1 on ending poverty in all its forms everywhere and the overarching goal of leaving no one behind cannot be achieved without considering the continued marginalisation of the LDCs. This chronic marginalisation is a fundamental development challenge as well as an opportunity that should be given more prominence in the contemporary global development discourse. The following sections will provide evidence for the disadvantaged dispositions of LDCs and the exogenous factors that contribute to them.

Africanisation of the LDCs

The profile of LDCs is being increasingly dominated by countries from the African continent. The LDC category began with 25 countries and saw 27 inclusions in subsequent years, with only four countries graduating since 1994 – Botswana (1994), Cape Verde (2007), the Maldives (2011) and Samoa (2014). According to the latest triennial review of 2015, of the 48 LDCs, 32 are African, one is Latin American (Haiti), eight are Asian and seven are Pacific islands countries. Since 2006, the number of African LDCs increased by one (South Sudan in 2015), while the number of Asian LDCs remains unchanged and the number of island LDCs decreased by three. The share of LDCs that are African will likely increase in the next 15 years, given a not-so-encouraging graduation outlook for this continent. Out of the countries in line for graduation by 2021, only two, Angola and Equatorial Guinea, are African countries (both of which are oil-producing), while the remaining seven – Bhutan, Kiribati, Nepal, São Tomé and Príncipe, the Solomon Islands, Timor-Leste, and Vanuatu – are either Pacific island or Asian countries.

In terms of accession to higher-income groups within the LDC category, only four of the 30 low-income African LDCs have moved to the middle- or high-income categories since 2006. In comparison, half of Asian LDCs and almost two-thirds of Pacific island LDCs are no longer among the low-income countries. As of 2015, 84% of low-income LDCs were African countries, or alternatively, of all African LDCs, 79% were low-income countries. Further aggravating the situation, approximately 36% of African LDCs are landlocked developing countries and 51.5% of African LDCs were in conflict.

Lack of convergence

Convergence is not happening between developed economies and LDCs. The gross domestic product (GDP) per capita figures (at USD 2005 constant prices) of developed countries and emerging economies have been converging since 2000. In contrast, the gap between the GDP per capita figure of LDCs as a group and that of other developing countries as a group has continued to widen (see Figure 5.1). Much of the progress within the LDCs group is by Pacific island countries, the average GDP per capita of which increased almost two-fold from an average of less than USD 800 in 2003-04 to more than USD 1 600 by 2014. Economic growth in African LDCs has slowed down and GDP per capita increased only marginally from an average of USD 413 in 2003 to USD 592 in 2014 owing to falling commodity prices as demand adjusted in China that affect the highly concentrated exports of African LDCs (Figure 5.1).

Figure 5.1. **GDP per capita in USD at constant prices (2005) and constant exchange rates (2005)**

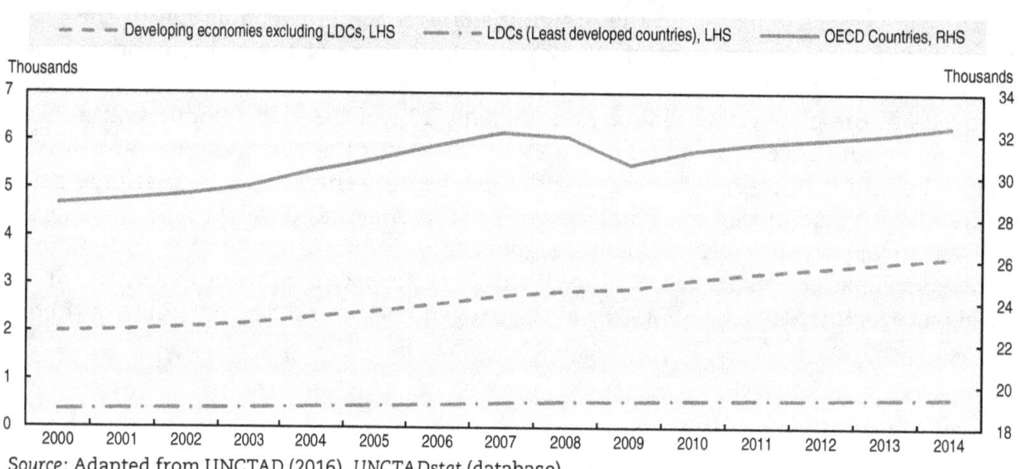

Source: Adapted from UNCTAD (2016), *UNCTADstat* (database).

Moreover, the Istanbul Programme of Action (IPoA) target of 7% GDP growth per year was met by only 11 LDCs in 2013 and eight LDCs in 2014, well below the average of 15 between 2001 and 2010 (UNOHRLLS, 2016). The comparable numbers for African LDCs stood at three in 2015 and an average of nine between 2003 and 2012. The economic growth rates in African LDCs have declined from an average of 6.1% over 2004-06 to an average of 3% over 2013-15 (World Bank, 2016b).The deceleration of GDP growth rates and consequently the slowdown of per capita income growth in African LDCs have further marginalised them not only in the global economy, but also among the LDCs.

Inequality and jobless growth

Besides slow and diverging GDP per capita growth rates, poverty and inequality remain high and economic growth has essentially been non-inclusive in LDCs – leading to greater income disparity and marginalisation. In its own turn, deepening of inequalities may have hampered these countries' growth prospects Between 2001 and 2012, an average of 51% of the LDC population lived below the international poverty line of USD 1.9 per day (constant 2011 purchasing power parity USD) (UN, 2016). There has been a meagre decrease of about 16.6% from the average poverty headcount ratio of 67.16% in the decade of

1981-91 when compared to the increase in average GDP per capita growth by 41.1% during the same period. Broken down by region, the poverty headcount ratio between 2001 and 2013 stood at an average of 55% for African LDCs (and Haiti) and 29.4% for Asian and Pacific island LDCs. Consistent with the trends in marginalisation, the share of the poor from African LDCs increased in both the global poor as well as the total LDC poor. Regarding inequality, out of 32 LDCs with available data on Gini coefficients for at least two points in time between 2000 and 2014, 14 LDCs have experienced a worsening situation over time (World Bank, 2016b). The phenomenon of jobless growth, where economies grow without creating proportionate levels of employment, has been apparent in almost all countries, as Dahlman and Mealy (2016) illustrate with the example of Bangladesh. A similar pattern is observed for LDCs as a group (Figure 5.2). Economic growth and employment levels grew at the same pace till 2000 after which employment growth diverged from GDP growth which essentially means it has been jobless and by implication non-inclusive.

Figure 5.2. **Jobless growth in LDCs**

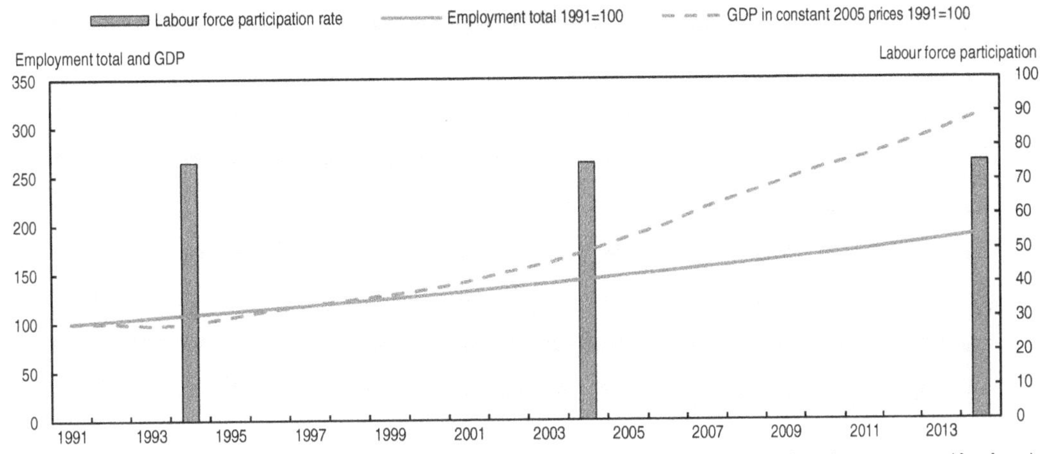

Source: Adapted from World Bank (2016b), *World Development Indicators* (database) and UNCTAD (2016), *UNCTADstat* (database).

Lack of diversification

Trade is an impetus for economic growth and employment creation in all countries including LDCs. Exports by LDCs as a share of global exports of goods and services almost doubled from 0.54% in 2000 to 1.02% in 2010, after which the growth rate slowed down and their share of global exports reached 1.1% in 2014 (UN-OHRLLS, 2016). Imports increased from 0.94% in 2000 to 1.73% in 2014 implying growing pressure on Balance of Payments. Compared to other developing countries, this progress is marginal and well below the 2% target advocated by the IPoA and SDGs. Moreover, in 2014, almost 70% of LDCs' merchandise exports remained concentrated on three major products (UN-OHRLLS, 2016). Although on a downward trend following the global financial crisis of 2008-09 and the subsequent fall in commodity prices, LDCs' exports are still highly specialised compared to two decades ago or with respect to other developing countries. These economies, usually very undiversified, have had low rates of manufacturing growth. More advanced economies have historically been characterised by more diversified export indices (Figure 5.3). Apart from being increasingly exposed to commodity price shocks, LDCs are also vulnerable to the emerging phenomenon of trade preference erosion (Keane, Aldafai and Arda, 2014).[4]

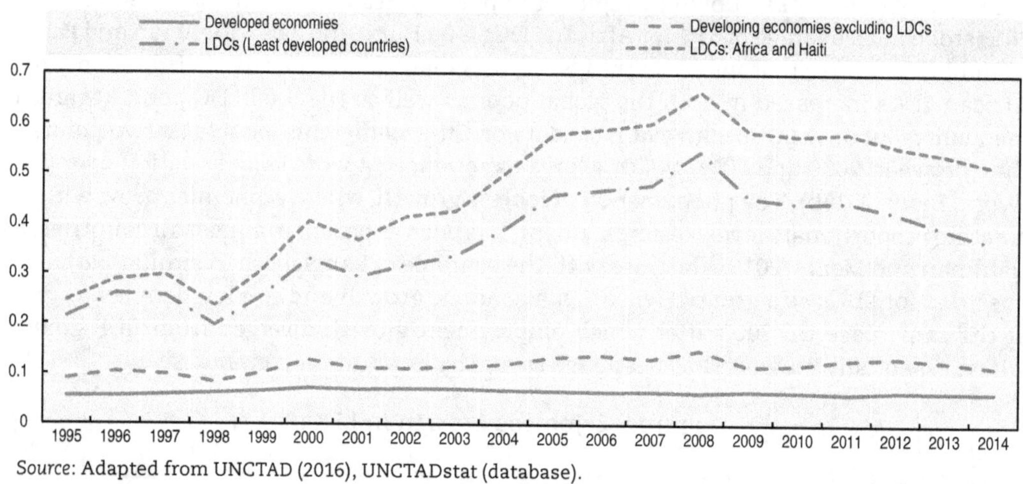

Figure 5.3. **Export concentration index**

Source: Adapted from UNCTAD (2016), UNCTADstat (database).

Resource flows

Foreign direct investment (FDI) can have a strong positive impact on upgrading export quality, while its effect on export diversification is higher in LDCs than non-LDCs (Gnangnon and Roberts, 2015). FDI inflows to LDCs exceeded foreign portfolio and other investments combined in 2001-10 and as such were the most important private capital flows (UNCTAD, 2011). While FDI inflows to LDCs rose rapidly from an estimated USD 7 billion in 2001 to USD 23.7 billion in 2010, they stagnated at USD 23.2 billion by 2014. The share of global FDI that LDCs received increased slightly from 1.01% in 2001 to 1.9% in 2014. When compared to other developing countries, the LDCs lag behind by a large and widening margin both in terms of total inflows and per capita inflows as a percentage of global FDI. Owing to the concentration of FDI flows to a few key resource-rich countries, African LDCs such as Mozambique, Zambia, Tanzania, the Democratic Republic of the Congo and Equatorial Guinea as well as Haiti accounted for 58% of total FDI to the LDCs in 2014 (Dahlman and Mealy, 2016).

The LDCs depend on official development assistance (ODA) for an average of 6% of their gross national income (GNI). Pacific island LDCs are comparatively more dependent on ODA, followed by African and Asian LDCs. For 14 LDCs in 2011-14, more than 50% of government expenditure came from ODA receipts and for five LDCs (Central African Republic, Democratic Republic of the Congo, Ethiopia, Rwanda and São Tomé and Príncipe) ODA accounted for expenses exceeding 100% (UN-OHRLLS, 2016 and WDI, 2016). ODA flows to LDCs increased by 4% in 2015 following several years of declining flows. However, ODA as a percentage of donor countries' GNI remained well below the commitment level of 0.15%. The honourable exception among them are the following eight out of the 29 DAC countries - Belgium, Denmark, Finland, Ireland, Luxembourg, Norway, Sweden and United Kingdom who met their commitments in 2014 (OECD, 2016b). It may be pointed out that demands for "results" and "value for money", as espoused by the ODA community, often impede higher disbursement of ODA, given the obtaining situation in the recipient countries. Further, the reallocation of ODA based on "geostrategic imperatives" (Dahlman and Mealy, 2016) towards conflict-afflicted areas characterised by war and refugee crises creates the potential to overlook under-aided LDCs and further marginalise them.

As far as mobilising domestic resources is concerned, LDCs are yet to breakout from their historically poor track record in this regard. Weak institutions, narrow tax bases, inefficient revenue collections and modest savings rate characterise LDCs' lacklustre progress (Bhattacharya and Akbar, 2014). Tax revenue as a percentage of GDP averaged 10% between 2000 and 2010 for LDCs compared to the world average of 14.7%. Moreover, budget deficit as a percentage of GDP in LDCs was estimated at -3.22% in 2015. It increased from an average of -0.53% between 2005 and 2010 to an average of -1.87% between 2011 and 2015.[5]

According to the Global Financial Integrity report (Kar, 2011), LDCs lost on average 60 cents in illicit financial flows for every dollar received in ODA over the period of 1990-2008. This forgone finance for development amounted to approximately USD 197 billion. Although large variations are likely to exist across countries, in any case, illicit flows are most probably understated owing to inadequate data.

Conflict situations

The geopolitical risks of interstate conflict, terrorist attacks, involuntary migration and refugee crises are significant contemporary global risks (WEF, 2016). As of 2016, 24 LDCs – 17 in Africa – were in a conflict or post-conflict situation, while 30 out of 48 LDCs – 23 in Africa – had at least one neighbouring country in conflict. In 2014, the unprecedented forced displacement of approximately 59.5 million people caused various stresses. Most migrants moved to other developing countries, thereby burdening already weak social and governance systems. Around 86% of refugees lived in developing countries and 12% lived in LDCs (IMF, 2016). Moreover, the majority of refugees are hosted by countries neighbouring their countries of origin (UNHCR, 2015).

External shocks

There are several impending global and regional challenges to the economies, societies and environment of the LDCs that increase the likelihood of their marginalisation. The LDCs', especially Africans', heavy dependence on commodities exports and natural resource rents, while their economies have remained undiversified and poorly industrialised, make them extremely vulnerable to the external shocks of fluctuating commodity prices. For example, oil prices dropped sharply by 51% in 2015, which affected oil-producing LDCs. Moreover, after peaking in 2011, commodity prices have declined rapidly since 2014. There was a 46% decline in agricultural raw materials and a 27.5% decline in food prices between 2011 and 2015 (UNOHRLLS, 2016).

In 2011-13, agricultural output constituted about 24.2% of GDP on average in LDCs and 25.2% of GDP in African LDCs. The agricultural labour force constituted 63% of the total labour force in LDCs in 2015 and is projected to comprise 61% by 2020. The proportion is greater for African LDCs, with 71% of the total labour force engaged in or looking for engagement in the agricultural sector in 2015 and projected to decrease by only 2% in 2020 (UNCTAD, 2016). Falling commodity prices remain a threat to sustainable, inclusive economic growth for the majority of LDCs even though few resource importing LDCs (e.g. Bangladesh) and net food importing developing countries benefitted from the price falls.

The faltering recovery of the world economy after the 2008-09 global financial and economic crisis did not help LDCs either. The volume of global trade grew slower than expected in 2015 by 2.7% and was roughly in line with GDP growth of 2.4%. Although growing in volume, the dollar value of LDCs merchandise exports fell by 14 % in 2015 (WTO, 2016). The sluggish global economy, along with China's dramatic economic slowdown, which is expected to deepen in 2017 (OECD, 2016a) has been another cause of stress for resource exporting LDCs. China's imports from Africa are expected to decline by 30% (UN-OHRLLS, 2016). This risk is compounded by the possibility of a protracted deterioration of growth prospects in developing countries, an economic downturn in key developed countries and an escalation of geopolitical tensions (World Bank, 2016a). There has been a global decline in import demand since 2014, as evidenced by the reduction of imports by developed countries from USD 10.5 trillion in 2014 to USD 9.2 trillion in 2015 and by developing countries from USD 7.7 trillion in 2014 to USD 6.7 trillion in 2015. Besides China, other emerging economies have been a substantial market for LDC exports and this downward trend has also affected them, thus exerting additional adverse pressure on the LDCs.

Climate change

The LDCs bear the impacts of climate change disproportionately, despite their less than 1% contribution to historical greenhouse gas emissions. Between 2010 and 2013, people living in LDCs were five times more likely to die from climate-related disasters than people living elsewhere (Craft, 2013). All 48 LDCs are considered vulnerable to climate change due to their incapacities to adapt. Moreover, the eight small island developing states as well as Asian countries like Myanmar, Bangladesh and Lao PDR are especially geographically and environmentally disadvantaged. The high incidence of poverty in LDCs compounds the already vulnerable situation of the LDC population. External support, both financial and technological, is crucial to combat large weather-related shocks and adapt to climate change (UN-OHRLLS, 2016).

Policy outlook

The various phenomena contributing to the marginalisation of LDCs, the impending external risks and their interconnections are illustrated in Figure 5.4.

Figure 5.4. **Factors and risks contributing to the marginalisation of the LDCs**

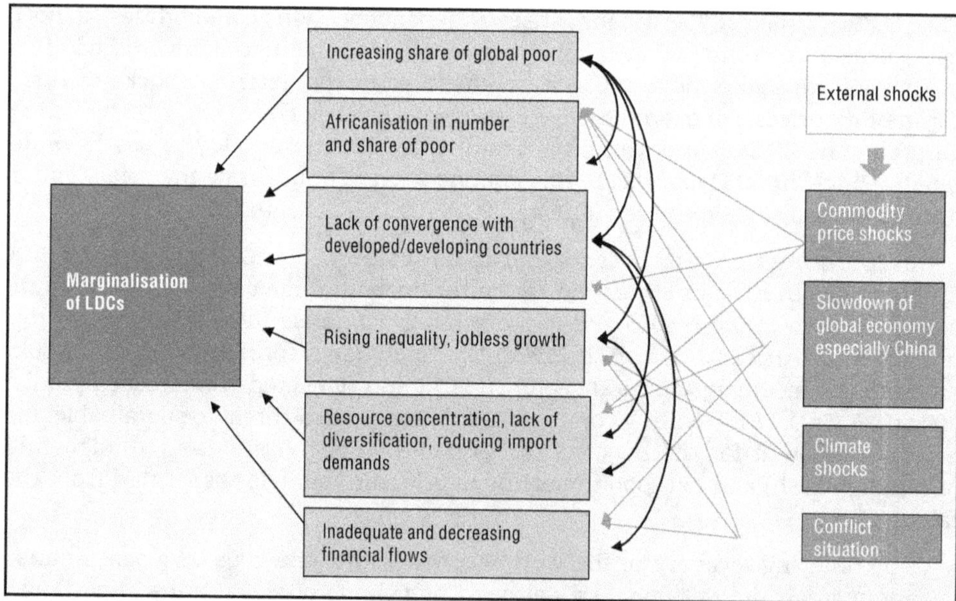

The global development discourse over the next 15 years needs to strongly acknowledge the risk of the LDCs being left behind. The achievement of the SDGs entails improved, innovative and continued international support for the LDCs, the progress of which should be the metric for meaningful transformation.

Based on the forgoing analyses, and in view of the new global development agenda, three key policy perspectives may be considered in the way forward for the least developed countries. First of all, LDCs need financial resources, access to technology and support for capacity development from the international development community. Their needs can be affectively serviced by fuller and faithful implementation of commitments made in the IPoA for least developed countries; especially by delivering on the IPoA target for the OECD's Development Assistance Committee countries to disburse between 0.15% and 0.2% of their gross national income exclusively to the LDCs. The Agenda 2030 for sustainable development, the Addis Ababa Action Agenda on finance for development, the World Trade Organization's Nairobi Package and the Paris Agreement on climate change are key commitments by the international community in the contemporary global development discourse. It is essential that synergies are drawn among these ambitious agendas. It is also important that ODA is increasingly leveraged to finance infrastructure, mobilising domestic resources and mitigating country-specific development impediments. Given the substantial development assistance that LDCs receive from the global South, which totals (33% of ODA received) (OECD, 2016b), the potential for triangular co-operation needs to be fully realised.

The global economy is increasingly favouring market mechanisms in lieu of non-market ones, which reiterates the importance of trade and investment. More liberal access to trade for LDCs is a must to engage in globally competitive export markets, foreign investment and global value chains. As such, there is a need to boost Aid for Trade, fully implement duty-free, quota-free market access (including reasonable rules of origin provisions) and eliminate non-tariff barriers. The LDCs have yet to gain 100% duty-free, quota-free market access for all products and existing privileges may be thwarted by ongoing trade negotiations among developed countries (UN-OHRLLS, 2016). Needless to say, protective mechanisms against any resulting preference erosion are necessary.

Second of all, LDCs require protection from the various systemic risks (e.g. lack of global economic and financial stability, commodities price shocks, climate change) they are exposed to. The SDG targets 17.13-17.15 on policy and institutional coherence in the global arena are especially pertinent in this regard. Development partners need to devise more effective arrangements and instruments to enhance global macroeconomic stability through increased co-ordination in the policy spectrum. Governments of both developed and developing countries need to consider impacts of their national policies and governance on individual country's policy space as legitimate platforms. With regard to finance for development in LDCs, combating the risk of illicit financial flows from the LDCs demands urgent cross-national, if not global, responses. There is need for international policy integration in the impending cross-sectoral reforms in the financial sector and tax regimes that should be accompanied by robust institutions and regulatory frameworks. Similarly, it is important to have coherence in the international communities' understanding of and approaches to LDCs in conflict situations.

Third of all, enabling domestic reforms must complement international support measures from development partners towards LDCs. LDCs need to actively take measures to strengthen capacities to address development challenges via institutional and policy reforms. For sustainable and inclusive growth, there is need for effective intervention in quite a few areas including: addressing infrastructure deficits, mobilising domestic taxes, improving the quality of public expenditure, promoting economic diversification in both exports and agriculture, and strengthening governance. Indeed, LDCs, in order to accelerate their transformative process also need to exploit full the potential of regional co-operation e.g. South-South. In the final analysis, LDCs themselves remain responsible for steering their journey on the development pathway.

Section 2. Revising ODA in the era of SDGs
Andrea Vignolo[6] and Karen Van Rompaey[7]

Discussions on the post-2015 development agenda have paved the way to new thinking about development as a multidimensional and global process. They also have built momentum for revising and modernising the concept and concessionality of Official Development Assistance (ODA).

ODA's eligibility and graduation criteria are still based fundamentally on countries' economic growth performance. A growing consensus among academic, practitioner and political communities[8] reveal that classifying countries according to their per capita income is inadequate to measure well-being or sustainability. Furthermore, it is not fit for the purpose of "leaving no one behind" in the era of universal sustainable development goals.

Achieving sustainable development is a far more complex enterprise than achieving economic growth. It requires not only the latter, but also specific knowledge, technologies, the right incentives and institutional capacities to change the way we currently live, work, produce, consume, share the fruits of growth and treat the planet. Otherwise, the quest towards economic growth can lead to negative consequences for the environment and future generations.

Middle- and upper-income developing countries have had access to an enhanced domestic resource base in the past decade to set forth their development priorities. They increasingly have assisted other developing countries through South-South and triangular co-operation. As a result of this growth in their aggregate income, some of them, like Antigua and Barbuda, Chile and Uruguay, have been classified recently as "high-income countries."

Is this just good news?

Despite past growth and progress in their human development indicators, most of these upper-income developing countries still face acute structural gaps and vulnerabilities that constitute persistent development bottlenecks. They need to close gaps in policies, institutions and capacities to ensure policy coherence towards sustainable development. They lag behind when it comes to accessing, for example, technologies and knowledge, both of which are the "game changers" required to transform their current model of growth into sustainable development (Bokova, 2012).

Moreover, the "rise of the South" has halted in Latin America and the Caribbean (LAC), threatening to jeopardise all progress made to date (UNDP, 2013). Currently, the LAC region is experiencing a slowdown in trade, a decrease in investment in physical infrastructure as well as human capital and innovation, and a reduction in fiscal space. External vulnerability remains very high since most of the economies in the region lack diversification and are vulnerable to climate change (Bárcenas, 2016).

Hence, ODA can play a strategic role to support these countries in the transition needed to build capacities in key areas/policy issues such as institutions, economic structures, risk management, social cohesion, research and innovation/technology to effectively achieve sustainable development.

Furthermore, by participating in triangular co-operation schemes, these developing countries can expand their contribution to global sustainable development by sharing their experiences, lessons learned and policy innovations.

Humankind stands at a critical juncture, when it is important to count on the contributions and support of all stakeholders to achieve the global sustainable development goals. It is therefore necessary to work towards an integral and non-exclusionary system of development co-operation that will fulfil the commitments made to date.

For an international co-operation system to be truly integral and non-exclusionary, it needs to provide the right incentives and overcome any zero-sum glance at the issues. While focusing on countries with greater challenges and less capacity to mobilise their own resources, ODA should support all developing countries according to their diverse conditions and needs. In this way, they can build their capacities and contribute towards global sustainable development.

Finally, it is thus necessary to review the OECD Development Assistance Committee's current ODA graduation criteria to include other multidimensional measures of well-being and sustainability beyond GNI and an alternative timeframe, according to the scale of both the challenges and commitments of Agenda 2030 for Sustainable Development.

Notes

1. Debapriya Bhattacharya (Ph.D) is a Distinguished Fellow at the Centre for Policy.

2. Sarah Sabin Khan is a Research Associate at the Centre for Policy Dialogue (CPD).

3. Although the PPP measure is used here to estimate poverty, we would like to mention that contemporary debates are moving towards other ways to measure multidimensional poverty like the MPI (Alkire and Santos, 2010; UNDP, 2010).

4. Most LDCs and some developing countries get exemptions or partial exemptions from standard developed country tariff rates. Preference margin is the difference between non-reciprocal preferential rates received by individual countries and the best available most favoured nation (MFN or better than MFN) treatment received on average by all other suppliers (Low et al, 2006). Trade negotiations that reduce standard developed country tariff rates erode the effective size of these preferences, and the competitive advantages they provide, and thus the term "preference erosion". This could happen even if the preferences themselves had not changed.

5. Budget deficits are calculated as the difference between general government revenue as a percentage of GDP and general government total expenditure as a percentage of GDP using data from World Economic Outlook (IMF, 2016).

6. Andrea Vignolo is the Executive Director of the Uruguayan Agency for International Co-operation.

7. Karen Van Rompaey is the Knowledge Manager of the Uruguayan Agency for International Co-operation.

8. See the growing consensus on par. 129 of the Addis Ababa Action Agenda on Financing for Development and on the Sustainable Development Goal 17.19; Dasgupta, P. (2016): "What's missing from the SDGs?", Global Views, Devex, available at https://goo.gl/1vqcBi; Alonso, J.A., Glennie, J. and Sumner, A. (2014): Receptores y contribuyentes: Los países de renta media y el futuro de la cooperación para el desarrollo, DESA Working Paper No. 135, Julio 2014; Tezanos, S. and Sumner, A. (2012): Beyond Low and Middle Income Countries: What if there were five clusters of developing countries?, IDS Working paper, Volume 2012 No. 404, IDS; Stiglitz, J., Sen, A. and Fitoussi, J.P (2010): "Mis-measuring our lives: Why GDP doesn't add up", The New York Press: London and Fleurbaey, M. (2009): "Beyond GDP: The quest for a measure of social welfare", Journal of Economic Literature, Vol. 47, Nr. 4, December 2009.

References

Alkire, S and M.E. Santos (2010), *Multidimensional Poverty Index*, Oxford Poverty and Human Development Initiative (OPHI) Briefing 01, http://www.ophi.org.uk/wp-content/uploads/OPHI-MPI-Brief.pdf.

Bárcenas, A. (2016), "Horizontes 2030: La igualdad en el centro del desarrollo sostenible". Trigésimo sexto período de sesiones de la CEPAL. 23 al 27 de mayo de 2016, Ciudad de México, http://www.cepal.org/es/publicaciones/40159-horizontes-2030-la-igualdad-centro-desarrollo-sostenible.

Bhattacharya D. and M.I. Akbar (2014), "Domestic resource mobilisation in the LDCs: Trends, determinants and challenges" in *Istanbul Programme of Action for the LDCs (2011–2020): Monitoring Deliverables, Tracking Progress – Analytical Perspectives*, Commonwealth Secretariat, London, http://ldc4monitor.org/wp-content/uploads/2015/06/istanbul-programme-of-action-for-the-ldcs-2011-2020-analytic-perspectives.pdf.

Bhattacharya, D. and T.I. Khan (2014), "The Challenges of Structural Transformation and Progress towards the MDGs in LDCs", in *Istanbul Program of Action for the LDCs (2011-2020): Monitoring Deliverables, Tracking Progress-Analytical Perspectives*, Commonwealth Secretariat, London, http://ldc4monitor.org/wp-content/uploads/2015/06/istanbul-programme-of-action-for-the-ldcs-2011-2020-analytic-perspectives.pdf.

Bokova, I. (2012), "An Integrated Policy Approach in Science, Technology, and Innovation for Sustainable Development: A UNESCO Idea in Action", *The Global Innovation Index 2012. Stronger Innovation Linkages for Global Growth*, INSEAD and WIPO, https://www.globalinnovationindex.org/userfiles/file/gii-2012-report.pdf.

Craft, B. (2013), "COP19: What the least developed countries expect from the climate talks", *The IIED blog*, www.iied.org/cop19-what-least-developed-countries-expect-climate-talks.

Dahlman, C. and S. Mealy (2016), "Obstacles to achieving the Sustainable Development Goals: Emerging global challenges and the performance of the least developed countries", in *Tracking Progress, Accelerating Transformations: Achieving the IPoA by 2020*, Commonwealth Secretariat, London, http://ldc4monitor.org/wp-content/uploads/2016/05/LDC-IV-Monitor.Tracking-Progress-Accelerating-Transformations-Achieving-IPoA-by-2020.pdf.

Francois, J., B. Hoekman and M. Manchin (2006), "Preference erosion and multilateral trade liberalization", *The World Bank Economic Review*, Vol. 20, No. 2, pp.197-216, https://www.tcd.ie/iiis/documents/discussion/pdfs/iiisdp87.pdf.

Gnangnon, S.K. and M. Roberts (2015), "Aid for trade, foreign direct investment and export upgrading in recipient countries", WTO *Working Paper*, ERSD-2015-10, World Trade Organisation, Geneva, www.wto.org/english/res_e/reser_e/ersd201510_e.pdf.

IMF (2016), *World Economic Outlook Database*, www.imf.org/external/pubs/ft/weo/2016/01/weodata/download.aspx (accessed 5 November 2016).

Kar, D. (2011)."Illicit financial flows from the least developed countries: 1990-2008." United Nations Development Programme, http://www.gfintegrity.org/wp-content/uploads/2014/05/IFFs_from_LDCs_web.pdf.

Keane, J., G. Aldafai and M. Arda (2014), "Structural economic transformation and export diversification in the least developed countries", in "Tracking progress, accelerating transformations: Achieving the IPoA by 2020", Commonwealth Secretariat, London, http://ldc4monitor.org/wp-content/uploads/2016/05/LDC-IV-Monitor.Tracking-Progress-Accelerating-Transformations-Achieving-IPoA-by-2020.pdf.

Low, P., R. Piermartini and J. Richtering (2006), *Non-reciprocal preference erosion arising from MFN liberalitzation in agriculture: What are the risks?*, World Trade Organisation Working Paper, Geneva, https://www.wto.org/english/res_e/reser_e/ersd200602_e.htm.

OECD (2016a), "China - Economic forecast summary (June 2016)", www.oecd.org/economy/china-economic-forecast-summary.htm (accessed 5 November 2016).

OECD (2016b), *OECD International Development Statistics* (database), http://dx.doi.org/10.1787/dev-data-en (accessed 5 November 2016).

UN (2016), "Implementation of the Programme of Action for the Least Developed Countries for the Decade 2011-2020", A/71/66–E/2016/11, United Nations, New York, http://unohrlls.org/about-ldcs/official-documents.

UNDP (2013), *Human Development Report 2013. The Rise of the South: Human Progress in a Diverse World*, UNDP, New York, http://hdr.undp.org/sites/default/files/reports/14/hdr2013_en_complete.pdf.

UNDP (2010), *Human Development Report 2010. The Real Wealth of Nations: Pathways to Human Development*, UNDP, New York. http://hdr.undp.org/sites/default/files/reports/270/hdr_2010_en_complete_reprint.pdf.

UN-OHRLLS (2016), "State of the least developed countries 2016", United Nations Office of the High Representative for the Least Developed Countries, Landlocked Developing Countries and Small Island Developing States, New York, http://unohrlls.org/custom-content/uploads/2016/08/State-of-LDCs2016.pdf.

UNCTAD (2016), *UNCTADstat* (database), http://unctadstat.unctad.org (accessed 5 November 2016).

UNCTAD (2015), "The Least Developed Countries Report 2015: Transforming Rural Economies", United Nations, New York, http://unctad.org/en/PublicationsLibrary/ldc2015_en.pdfUNHCR (UN High Commissioner for Refugees) (2015) *World at War. Forced Displacement in 2014.* New York and Geneva: UNHCR, http://www.unhcr.org/556725e69.pdf.

UNCTAD (2011), "Foreign direct investment in LDCs: Lessons learned from the decade 2001–2010 and the way forward", UNCTAD/DIAE/IA/2011/1, United Nations Conference on Trade and Development, Geneva, http://unctad.org/en/Docs/diaeia2011d1_en.pdf.

WEF (2016), "The global risks report 2016", World Economic Forum, Geneva, www3.weforum.org/docs/GRR/WEF_GRR16.pdf.

World Bank (2016a), "Global economic prospects: Divergences and risks", Washington, DC, http://pubdocs.worldbank.org/en/842861463605615468/Global-Economic-Prospects-June-2016-Divergences-and-risks.pdf.

World Bank (2016b), *World Development Indicators* (database), http://data.worldbank.org/indicator (accessed 5 November 2016).

World Trade Organization (2016), *World Trade Statistical Review 2016*, https://www.wto.org/english/res_e/statis_e/wts2016_e/wts2016_e.pdf.

Author biographies

Chapter 2

Alan Hirsch is Professor of Development Policy and Practice and has directed the Graduate School of Development Policy and Practice at UCT since 2013. He was born in Cape Town and educated in Economics, Economic History and History at UCT, Wits and Columbia. After teaching economic history and economics at the University of Cape Town, he joined the South African Department of Trade and Industry in 1995, managing industry and technology policy. He worked at the South African Presidency from 2002 to 2012 where he managed economic policy, represented the Presidency at the G20, and was co-chair of the G20 Development Working Group. He has served or serves on the boards of a range of research or training centres including the European Centre for Development Policy Management. He was a visiting scholar at the Harvard Business School, was a regular visiting professor at the Graduate School of Governance at Maastricht University, directed the International Growth Centre's research in Zambia for 5 years, and was a member of the OECD secretary-general's Inclusive Growth Advisory Panel. He writes about economic development issues, including *Season of Hope - Economic Reform under Mandela and Mbeki* and recently co-edited *The Oxford Companion to South African Economics*.

Donald Mmari is an economist with vast experience in development planning, policy analysis, socio-economic research, and institutional development. He holds a Ph.D from the International Institute of Social Studies of Erasmus University Rotterdam, an MBA from University of Oregon and an MA (Economics) from the University of Dar es Salaam. He has been actively involved in the preparation of national development policies, including National Strategy for Growth and Reduction of Poverty, the Natural Gas Policy of Tanzania in 2012 and the Second Five Year Development Plan in 2015/16. He has published articles, working papers, policy briefs, and research reports on the extractives sector, manufacturing, governance, social protection, and on export competitiveness of agricultural commodities. He has actively engaged the co-ordination of research and analysis working group and preparation of Tanzania poverty and human development reports from 2001 to 2011. Dr. Mmari has immense economic policy and management experience accumulated over the years of his various positions within REPOA and outside, and membership in the Board of Directors of public entities. He is currently the Executive Director of REPOA.

Neuma Grobbelaar is an experienced foreign policy and development expert with 28 years of specialist research, project, research management, fundraising and policy practioner experience. A former South African diplomat, she is the research director of the South African Institute of International Affairs (SAIIA), a leading African Foreign policy think tank based at the University of the Witwatersrand. Her areas of research specialisation include the intersection between foreign policy, regional integration and human development; the role of the private sector in African development initiatives and South Africa's role as an emerging development partner in Africa. She holds an MPhil in Economic Policy from the University of Stellenbosch; a Master in Art History from the University of Glasgow and an Honours in Business Administration and International Relations from the University of Pretoria.

Vugar Bayramov is a well-known economist in Azerbaijan. He was a visiting faculty member at Washington University (USA) in 2002/2004. Mr. Bayramov has a Ph.D. in economics. His papers/books have been translated into 25 languages. In 2010, Mr. Bayramov was named one of the 500 most influential Muslims in the world by The Royal Islamic Strategic Studies Centre (RISSC) in Jordan. Mr. Bayramov has served as Co-chair at the EU Eastern Partnership Civil Society Forum in 2013/2014. He was the co-coordinator of the Economic Integration and Convergence to EU Standards Working Group at the EaP CSF in 2011-2012. Mr. Bayramov is the chairman of Centre for Economic and Social Development (CESD, www.cesd.az). According to the University of Pennsylvania Global

Think Tanks Rankings, the Centre has been selected as a top think tank in Southern Caucasus and Central Asia for the last five years.

Ahmad Alili is a Senior Researcher at the Centre for Economic and Social Development (CESD). He has a Master's Degree in International Public Policy from University College London. Mr. Alili is conducting qualitative and quantitative research on the economies of developing countries, foreign policy and conflicts. Mr. Alili has gained experience in governmental and non-governmental organisations dealing with developing country economies, international relations and conflicts. He has authored and edited various handbooks and published analytical articles on conflicts and international relations for local media outlets on a regular basis.

Chapter 3

René N'Guettia Kouassi holds: i) a Ph.D in Economics and (ii) a specialised Ph.D in Development Economics. As supplementary training, he also holds Advanced Studies Diplomas in Economics and in Land Use Planning. He is currently Director of the Economic Affairs Department of the African Union Commission, a post he has held since July 2004. Prior to that, he was Director of Deputy Cabinet to the Secretary General of the OAU, Dr. Salim Ahmed Salim and Director of the Office of the Acting President of the AU Commission, Mr Amara Essy. He also co-ordinated the African Institute for Economic Development and Planning (IDEP) program on industrial development in Africa from 1996 to 1997. Additionally he technically coordinates the implementation of the African Charter on Statistics, the Strategy for the Harmonization of Statistics (SHaSA), the Minimum Integration Program (PMI), and the Microfinance Action Plan.

Gilbert Houngbo is currently the Deputy Director-General of the International Labour Organization (since March 2013), leading the Organization's field operations in more than 100 countries as well as its bilateral and multilateral partnerships. Mr. Houngbo is the former Prime Minister of Togo (2008-2012). He led the government towards substantial improvements in the achievement of Togo's MDG targets, and towards enhancements in the rule of law and civil liberties. He introduced economic reforms, including the Highly Indebted Poor Countries (HIPC) program of the International Monetary Fund and implemented national policies focused on broad-based economic growth. Mr Houngbo held the position of Assistant Secretary General, preceded by a number of senior executive posts at the United Nations Development Programme (1996-2008). As UNDP Regional Director for Africa, he led UNDP poverty alleviation programmes in sub-Saharan Africa with offices in 45 countries and annual delivery exceeding USD 1 billion.

Samir Saran (Ph. D) spearheads the Observer Research Foundation (ORF) outreach and business development activities, and heads the ORF Global Governance and Cyber and Media programmes. He is the founding Chair of *CyFy: The India Conference on Cyber Security and Internet Governance*, Co-Convener of the India-U.S. Track 1.5 Cyber Dialogue, a member of the WEF Global Future Council on Cybersecurity, and Director, Centre for Peace & Conflict Studies, Sardar Patel University of Police, Security and Criminal Justice. He co-created and launched India's first "green stock exchange" and has published extensively on climate change, development, energy, Internet, radicalism and is a student of matters 'global governance'.

Vivan Sharan leads Koan Advisory's macro-advisory and regulatory practice in New Delhi. He is an economist with diverse experience in the policy circuit. Previously, he has served as the Chief Executive of the Global Governance programme at the Observer Research Foundation (ORF) and as the Business Head of a sustainability company that ran India's first energy efficiency index on the Bombay Stock Exchange. A former financial markets professional, his diverse subject interests include competition, technology and IPR. He is a Visiting Fellow at ORF where he is involved with research on the digital economy.

Hussein Al-Majali is Executive Vice Chairman, Middle East and North Africa at Magellan Global Advisers. Prior to co-founding Magellan, Hussein served in a variety of leadership roles in the Jordanian Government and military for over 30 years before retiring at the rank of a four-star general. He served as Minister of the Interior and Minister for Municipal Affairs between 2013 and 2015 and was previously Head of the Jordanian Police Service, Ambassador to Bahrain and Commander of the Royal Guards Brigade.

Chapter 4

Sanjayan Velautham (Ph.D) was appointed Executive Director of the ASEAN Centre for Energy in January 2015. Dr. Velautham has more than 25 years of experience in the industry, academia and research institutes. A registered professional engineer with a doctoral degree in Engineering, he has 15 years in the energy industry, and 10 years of research/teaching experience at Kyushu University, Japan, and University Technology Malaysia.

Tian Huifang (Ph.D) is the Deputy Director and Senior Research Fellow at the Department of Global Governance at the Institute of World Economics and Politics, Chinese Academy of Social Sciences, with the research fields of environmental economics and development economics, global governance and CGM modelling. She was also the visiting scholar at University of Toronto in 2014, University of Gothenburg in Sweden in 2012, and University of Western Ontario in Canada in 2008-2009. She has published many academic papers in some SSCI and top-level journals like "Journal of Policy Modeling", "Climate Change Economics", "China and World Economy", etc. The scientific research projects she was and now is in charge of, include the National Social Sciences Fund Major Project, the APEC "Green Finance" project, the Economic Research Institute for ASEAN and East Asia (ERIA) "Circular Economy" project, amongst others.

Chapter 5

Debapriya Bhattacharya (Ph.D), a macro-economist and public policy analyst, is currently a Distinguished Fellow at the Centre for Policy Dialogue (CPD) in Dhaka. He is a former Ambassador and Permanent Representative of Bangladesh to the World Trade Organization offices in Geneva and Vienna, and the Special Advisor on Least Developed Countries (LDCs) to the Secretary General of the UN Conference on Trade and Development (UNCTAD). He is associated with a number of leading institutions, networks and editorial boards of reputed journals. Dr. Bhattacharya has studied in Dhaka, Moscow and Oxford, and held a number of visiting positions, including at the Centre for Global Development (CGD), Washington DC. He is the chair of two global networking initiatives, LDC IV Monitor and Southern Voice on Post-MDG International Development Goals.

Sarah Sabin Khan is a Research Associate at the Centre for Policy Dialogue (CPD), Bangladesh. She has a Master of Arts degree in Economics from McGill University, Canada and a Bachelor's of Business Administration degree with dual majors in Finance and Economics from North South University, Bangladesh. Prior to joining CPD, she had worked with a foreign aid supported market development project and at a consultancy firm specialised in power sector development. Ms. Sarah Khan's current research interests include international development co-operation and empirical microeconometrics.

Andrea Vignolo is the Executive Director of the Uruguayan Agency for International Co-operation since 2015. She has 20 years' experience in the public sector (national and local government) and academic realm of international co-operation at both advisory and managerial levels. Andrea was trained as a psychologist at the Universidad de la República in Uruguay.

Karen Van Rompaey is the Knowledge Manager of the Uruguayan Agency for International Co-operation since its creation in 2010 and has been working in this field from different angles: public sector, donor agency, civil society and university. She holds an MA in International Political Economy from Warwick University in the UK.

ORGANISATION FOR ECONOMIC CO-OPERATION AND DEVELOPMENT

The OECD is a unique forum where governments work together to address the economic, social and environmental challenges of globalisation. The OECD is also at the forefront of efforts to understand and to help governments respond to new developments and concerns, such as corporate governance, the information economy and the challenges of an ageing population. The Organisation provides a setting where governments can compare policy experiences, seek answers to common problems, identify good practice and work to co-ordinate domestic and international policies.

The OECD member countries are: Australia, Austria, Belgium, Canada, Chile, the Czech Republic, Denmark, Estonia, Finland, France, Germany, Greece, Hungary, Iceland, Ireland, Israel, Italy, Japan, Korea, Latvia, Luxembourg, Mexico, the Netherlands, New Zealand, Norway, Poland, Portugal, the Slovak Republic, Slovenia, Spain, Sweden, Switzerland, Turkey, the United Kingdom and the United States. The European Union takes part in the work of the OECD.

OECD Publishing disseminates widely the results of the Organisation's statistics gathering and research on economic, social and environmental issues, as well as the conventions, guidelines and standards agreed by its members.

OECD DEVELOPMENT CENTRE

The OECD Development Centre was established in 1962 as an independent platform for knowledge sharing and policy dialogue between OECD member countries and developing economies, allowing these countries to interact on an equal footing. Today, 27 OECD countries and 25 non-OECD countries are members of the Centre. The Centre draws attention to emerging systemic issues likely to have an impact on global development and more specific development challenges faced by today's developing and emerging economies. It uses evidence-based analysis and strategic partnerships to help countries formulate innovative policy solutions to the global challenges of development.

For more information on the Centre and its members, please see www.oecd.org/dev.

OECD PUBLISHING, 2, rue André-Pascal, 75775 PARIS CEDEX 16

(41 2017 05 1 P) ISBN 978-92-64-27314-6 – 2017